Deck guides us to the kind of business and organization
…s been the secret to long run success. Someone once
…-fiction gives us knowledge but fiction gives wisdom.
…s even more powerful than either because it tells a story
…I with real wisdom from giants of business. And although
…easy read it gives us all the tools to move to a culture
…ship that can withstand and prosper in the most difficult
…s. Joe Tye draws on the best business literature and his own
…tial experience to show how work in groups can be generative
…v possibilities in work and life. I've already gone back to this
…several times and am using it in my own work. Start your new
…ney with this book and keep it at your side."

—Michael L. Ray, Stanford Graduate School of Business,
Author, *Creativity in Business, The Highest Goal,*
and co-editor, *The New Paradigm in Business*

"In *All Hands On Deck*, Joe Tye takes us on an Alice in Wonder-
land journey to observe some of history's most successful leaders
in action. With this dramatic technique, Tye reveals again the too-
often-forgotten principles of leadership, how they are made real in
the workplace, and the results they produce. This is a teaching tale
that also entertains. I highly recommend this book to those who want
to be leaders and to leaders who want a refresher course."

—James A. Autry, Author, *The Servant Leader*

"Joe Tye teaches us through great business leaders of the past, the key
steps to creating a culture of ownership. Great lessons, well told and
easy to read. Get your hands on a copy, read it, and put the lessons to
work. Whether you are a CEO or lead a team of two, each lesson is
relevant, applicable, and yours for the taking. Thanks for an inspiring
and important book, Joe!"

—Kevin Eikenberry, Author of *Remarkable Leadership:
Unleashing Your Leadership Potential One Skill at a Time*

All Hands On Deck

All
Hands
On
Deck

8 Essential Lessons
for Building a
Culture of Ownership

Joe Tye

WILEY

John Wiley & Sons, Inc.

Published by John Wiley & Sons, Inc., Hoboken, New Jersey.
Published simultaneously in Canada.

For general information on our other products and services or for technical support, please contact our
Customer Care Department within the United States at (800) 762-2974, outside the United States at
(317) 572-3993 or fax (317) 572-4002.

Wiley also publishes its books in a variety of electronic formats. Some content that appears in print
may not be available in electronic books. For more information about Wiley products, visit our web
site at www.wiley.com.

Library of Congress Cataloging-in-Publication Data:

Tye, Joe.
    All hands on deck: 8 essential lessons for building a culture of ownership/by Joe Tye.
        p. cm.
    Includes bibliographical references.
    ISBN 978-0-470-59912-9 (cloth); ISBN 978-0-470-63747-0 (ebk);
ISBN 978-0-470-63748-7 (ebk); ISBN 978-0-470-63749-4
    1. Corporate culture. 2. Organizational behavior. 3. Employee motivation.
4. Management—Employee participation. I. Title.
    HD58.7.T94 2010
    658.4′063—dc22
                                                                    2010000760

Printed in the United States of America

10 9 8 7 6 5 4 3 2 1

For Sally, who puts the wind in my sails on the open seas and keeps me anchored in the storms.

Contents

When you look at your people, do you see costs to be reduced? Do you see recalcitrant employees prone to opportunism, shirking, and free riding who can't be trusted and who need to be closely controlled through monitoring, rewards, and sanctions? Do you see people performing activities that can and should be contracted out to save on labor costs? Or, when you look at your people, do you see intelligent, motivated, trustworthy individuals—the most critical and valuable strategic assets your organization can have? When you look at your people, do you see them as the fundamental resources on which your success rests and the primary means of differentiating yourself from the competition? Perhaps even more importantly, would someone observing how your organization manages its people recognize your point of view in what you do as opposed to what you talk about doing?

—Jeffrey Pfeffer, *The Human Equation: Building Profits by Putting People First*

(Boston, MA: Harvard Business School Press, 1998, p. 292)

Foreword

One day in 1999, as I was giving a presentation for a group of independent insurance agents who represent Auto-Owners Insurance Company, we kept being interrupted by this awful racket from the room next door. At the next break, I went to check out this source of annoyance. The speaker at the front of the room was leading two hundred or so seemingly respectable businesspeople as they were jumping up and down and roaring like hungry lions. I listened to the speaker for a while then, rather than asking him to hold down the noise (which had been my original intention), I invited him to visit Auto-Owners headquarters for a retreat with our senior leadership team. That was the beginning of a long relationship between Auto-Owners Insurance and Values Coach, and a lasting friendship between Joe Tye and me.

I'm pleased to write a foreword for this book for two reasons beyond my friendship with the author. First, while the story itself is fictional, the underlying principles are fundamental to building an enduring organization. At Auto-Owners, a culture of ownership is woven right into our DNA, and our practices reflect the lessons described in this book. We take our central purpose and our 10 core values very seriously. We expect our associates to know what those 10 values are and to buy into the expectations those values create. Over the years, Joe has randomly stopped hundreds of our associates and asked them to recite our values. Almost everyone is able to do it.

We are very proud of the fact that in our nearly one hundred years of operation—through two world wars, the Great Depression and multiple recessions, and the great restructuring frenzy—Auto-Owners has never had a layoff. We almost always promote from within, and every one of our senior officers has devoted his or her career to the company. Our culture of ownership is reflected in the fact that our employee turnover is substantially less than the industry average, while our productivity per employee is substantially higher than the industry average. It's also reflected in the fact that for the past two years, J.D. Power has ranked Auto-Owners as number one for customer satisfaction in automobile claims.

As is the case with the companies described in this book, our commitment to fostering that spirit of ownership extends beyond the boundaries of our organization. We consider the independent insurance agents who sell and service our products to be true partners in our business, and we have maintained a steadfast loyalty to the agency system for close to a century. In this, our philosophy is very similar to that of Ray Kroc toward his suppliers and franchisees or of Mary Kay Ash toward her independent beauty consultants. When I read about the family picnics hosted by Bill Hewlett and Dave Packard, I was immediately reminded of Auto-Owners family nights at the stadium where the Lansing Lugnuts play baseball.

The second reason I'm pleased to write this foreword is that over the past 10 years, Joe has given presentations for our 3,400 associates and thousands of our independent insurance agents across the county. His message of building a culture of ownership on a foundation of values is more important today than ever before. Whether you are a Fortune 500 company or an independent insurance agency, a large hospital or a community clinic, a big university or a local nonprofit agency, you must learn and apply these eight essential lessons if you want to build an organization that endures and creates a legacy that lasts.

—Roger Looyenga
Chairman and CEO (retired), Auto-Owners Insurance Company

(*Auto-Owners Insurance is a Fortune 500 company headquartered in Lansing, Michigan. You can see the company's 10 core values at* www.Auto-Owners.com.)

Acknowledgments

This book is a result of my work with Values Coach over the past fifteen years. I'm grateful to the clients that have entrusted us to help them work toward a culture of ownership, and to all of the individuals who have participated in our courses on values-based life and leadership skills. Auto-Owners Insurance Company is the best example I know of a culture of ownership in action, and I greatly appreciate Roger Looyenga for gracing this book with a foreword. Alden Solovy is a valued supporter and hiking buddy, and I'm thankful to him for introducing me to the terrific team at the American Hospital Association, including Neil Jesuele, Laura Woodburn, Connie Lang, Dave Parlin, Dr. John Combes, and the rest of the crew at Health Forum. Patrick Charmel, Susan Frampton and their colleagues at Planetree are changing the face of healthcare, and it's a privilege for Values Coach to sponsor the bookstore at their annual conference.

In the Values Coach office, it's a blessing to have the support of a committed and enthusiastic team including Paula Yrigoyen, Michelle Arduser, Thuy Do, Hung Viet Tran, Tung Hoang, and the irreplaceable Sally Bonkers. Dick Schwab is a valued coach and colleague. I appreciate the members of our Advisory Board for always pushing us to see a bigger picture and go after bigger goals.

The publishing team at John Wiley & Sons has been a joy to work with. I'm forever grateful that Lauren Lynch sent me an e-mail asking if I had another book in me, and then helped me move from a vague "I think so" to completing the book you now have in your hands. Deborah Schindlar, Lindsay Morgan, Peter Knox, and the rest of the Wiley production team helped shape, polish, and promote this book.

Peter Miller and Adrienne Rosado of PMA Literary and Film Management are the best representatives an author could ask for.

Behind every great conference there's a hardworking and often underappreciated meeting planner, and I appreciate them all! I also appreciate the speakers bureaus it's my privilege to work with, including Five Star Speakers and Trainers, The Tiller Group, BigSpeak!, Otellus, Midwest Speakers Bureau, Executive Speakers Bureau, and Health Forum Faculty.

Most important, I want to acknowledge my family. My parents Joe and Janelle have been unstinting in their support over the years, as have my brothers, Steven and Allen, and my sister Nancy. I could not be more proud of my son Doug, on his way to becoming an English professor, and daughter Annie, who is breaking new ground in neurobiology research. And finally, this book is dedicated to my best friend and life partner, Sally.

Introduction

Why a Culture of Ownership Matters

Culture eats strategy for lunch! Enron had a brilliant business strategy, but the company was brought down by a fatally flawed corporate culture. During the 1990s, IBM was rescued from a fatally flawed business strategy by a process that revitalized the spirit of the company's original culture. Given this business truism, it is surprising that so much executive energy goes into creating strategy and so little goes into changing the cultural attitudes and behaviors that are essential to fulfill those strategies. As David Maister points out in his book *Strategy and the Fat Smoker: Doing What's Obvious but Not Easy* (Boston: Spangle Press, 2008), most of us know what we should be doing; the challenge is motivating ourselves, and others, to do those things—in other words, to inspire people to take ownership.

Likewise, it is surprising that not very many business leaders put as much effort into designing and building the "invisible architecture" of corporate culture as they do the visible architecture of their physical facilities. We would not so much as remodel a bathroom

without a detailed blueprint describing where every electrical out-
let goes, but we allow culture to evolve haphazardly and without
plan or design. As just one example, every organization we work
with at Values Coach Inc. claims "integrity" as a core value, at
least implicitly. Yet, every single one of them has a rumor mill (so
does yours, I'm willing to bet). Gossip (along with complaining,
finger-pointing, passive-aggressiveness, and other forms of toxic
emotional negativity) is tolerated in the way we once tolerated
cigarette smoking. As Lori Palatnik and Bob Burg point out in their
book *Gossip: Ten Pathways to Eliminate It from Your Life and Transform
Your Soul* (Deerfield Beach, FL: Simcha Press, 2002), gossip violates
the dignity of the person being gossiped about. More important,
it violates the integrity of those doing the gossiping—and of those
who allow there to be a culture that tolerates toxic emotional negativity in the first place. Appendix 1 includes a suggested approach
to crafting a cultural blueprint.

The knee-jerk reaction to behavioral problems in the workplace is to try to "hold people accountable." This rarely works
for very long, and sometimes backfires, because accountability is
an externally imposed expectation, not something for which the
person being held accountable has taken ownership (hence the
need to have his or her "feet held to the fire"). The truth is that
you cannot hold people accountable for the things that really matter in an organization. Loyalty, enthusiasm, pride, courage, care,
and similar qualities are of the heart, not the head. Accountability
can only create extrinsic motivation: fear of punishment and/or
hope for reward. It takes a sense of ownership to spark intrinsic
motivation. When there is a culture of ownership, people do their
best work because they expect it of themselves, not because someone else is looking over their shoulder (or holding their feet to
the fire).

Shortly after the federal government's bank bailout, I heard a radio interview in which the CEO of one of the nation's largest investment banks justified six- and seven-figure bonuses being paid to "the best and the brightest" by saying that if they didn't receive those payments, they would leave for more money elsewhere. This, he implied, is the way of the capitalist world. He was wrong. That is *not* the way of the capitalist; it is the way of the mercenary (and the prostitute). Without exception, the leaders featured in *All Hands on Deck* spent most or all of their careers with the same organization. They were committed to the success of their organizations and to the careers of the people who worked for those organizations. They did not jump ship when times got tough or when they thought they could make more money elsewhere. They were builders, not takers. The same is true of the people who are building today's greatest organizations; Steve Jobs, Bill Gates, Jeff Bezos, Gary Keller (Keller Williams Realty), Tom Frist (HCA), Kent Taylor (Texas Roadhouse), Wendy Kopp (Teach for America), and people like them are committed to the mission, not the money. And *that* is the true way of capitalism.

A Culture of Ownership Is Essential for Great Customer Service

A culture of ownership is the sine qua non of great customer service. It is the difference between creating raving fans and provoking outraged activists. In a world where an angry customer can literally reach millions of people overnight, no company can afford to have employees who are just renting their jobs, treating customers in a manner that conveys that they don't care. As of this writing, more than eight million people have watched singer David Carroll's

YouTube video "United Breaks Guitars" (it will be a lot more by the time you read this). This is the last sort of publicity the struggling air carrier needs; had one single United customer service agent taken ownership for the problem, this incredible public relations black eye would never have happened. Nordstrom department stores can have an employee policy manual that's only two sentences long ("Use good judgment in all situations. There will be no additional rules.") because their people have a sense of ownership for the company's values, mission, and practices.

An ownership culture is especially critical for effective service recovery. Let me illustrate with two personal stories. While working on this book, I replaced my original Kindle wireless reading device with the newer model. After several weeks, the screen froze. I sent an e-mail to the Amazon.com service desk, and within five minutes I was on the phone with someone who walked me through the steps to reset the device. When that was unsuccessful, he arranged to have a new Kindle sent to me via FedEx, including a prepaid box for returning the defective unit. He did not need to get a supervisor's approval; he acted like an owner and made a decision on the spot. As a result, I am now more than ever a raving fan of both Amazon.com and my Kindle.

Contrast that with the experience I had after Lasik surgery left me with double vision, impaired visual acuity, and chronic eye pain. The surgery was performed by one of the largest eye clinics in the Midwest—one that advertises itself as having some of the best doctors in the country. Yet, trying to get someone from the clinic to give me an explanation as to why I had such a bad outcome, much less to help me cope with the serious problems caused by the surgery, was about as productive as trying to communicate with a dead bug. I was eventually so frustrated that I filed a complaint with the state board of medicine, and I posted a video on YouTube *(Before You Let Them Cut on Your Eyes)* using my experience to warn anyone considering this surgery about how the economics of the Lasik industry can lead to being given a dishonest diagnosis and inappropriate surgery and to being abandoned if extensive follow-up care is required. All I wanted from the clinic was for someone to take ownership for the problems they created. Because no one would, I am now an angry activist who is determined to reach a large audience with this warning.

A Culture of Ownership Enhances Operating Effectiveness

What gets measured gets done. Under the banner of that mantra, corporate America has launched one campaign of accountability after another. Total quality management, six sigma, just-in-time, lean (and mean) and other such programs are intended to boost productivity, reduce quality variations, eliminate defects, and help people "do more with less." Such left-brain tactics are necessary but not sufficient to create a great organization. Productivity and quality can be as much, if not more, influenced by how enthusiastically people approach their work (and the spaces in between actually doing that work) as they are by the processes that have been designed for that work.

Appendix 2 of this book includes *The Self-Empowerment Pledge*. Take a minute to read the seven simple promises that make up that pledge (responsibility, accountability, determination, contribution, resilience, perspective, and faith). Then, ask yourself how much more effectively your people would get their work done, serve your customers, and support one another if everyone made a good-faith effort to live those promises. As an added benefit, think about how much better their own personal, professional, and family lives would be. I've shared The Pledge with thousands of people; for those who really take it to heart, the results are often nothing short of miraculous. A culture of ownership begins with empowered people, but empowerment is always an inside job. You cannot empower people; you can only inspire them to empower themselves.

A Culture of Ownership Gives Stability during Challenging Times

Each of the companies whose founding leaders are featured in this book endured challenging times and in every case were able to survive and even thrive during those times largely because of the stability provided by people who felt a sense of ownership. During the Great Depression (that hardest of hard times), IBM, Hewlett-Packard, 3M, and Disney not only survived without resorting to layoffs, but they all continued to grow. It is precisely during tough times that an organization needs the greatest courage, creativity, commitment, and effort from its people, and these qualities are a by-product of building a culture of ownership.

In the days immediately following the tragedy of 9/11, the airline industry had a collective panic attack and almost immediately laid off more than one hundred thousand workers. As a result of this managerial cowardice, the economic impact of the terrorist attacks was greatly magnified. The only major air carrier to stand firm was Southwest Airlines, which is justly famous for its culture of ownership. Over the next several years, most of the major airlines went through bankruptcy. The exception was Southwest, which continued to grow—largely at the expense of those that had chosen to shrink. Southwest was able to face the crisis with confidence because its people had shown their commitment to the company (their spirit of ownership) in every previous crisis.

(For more about Southwest Airlines' culture of ownership, see the book *Nuts! Southwest Airlines' Crazy Recipe for Business and Personal Success* [Austin, TX: Bard Books, 1996] by Kevin and Jackie Freiberg.)

A Culture of Ownership Creates Bonds of Loyalty

Our economy is headed into a perfect storm on the employment front. To paraphrase the subtitle of Roger Herman's book *Impending Crisis* (Winchester, VA: Oakhill Press, 2002), there will be too many jobs chasing too few people. Over the next 10 years or so, some seventy million baby boomers will exit the workforce, and only forty million new workers will come from the next generational cohort to replace them. At the same time, globalization, new technology, and expanded alternatives for work and lifestyle will make it increasingly difficult for the traditional company to recruit and retain great people. In his book *The 2010 Meltdown: Solving the Impending Jobs Crisis* (Westport, CT: Praeger Publishers, 2005), Edward E. Gordon writes, "Throughout the entire economy, the United States lacks adequate numbers of appropriately skilled workers to support high standards in personal or professional services, or properly maintain the physical and technological infrastructure upon which everyone relies and takes for granted" (p. 17).

A company can attract people with left-brain inducements such as pay and benefits, job titles, promises of advancement, and the like. But those people will stay because they like the people they are working with and for, they are proud of the work they do, and they feel like what they are doing is important. In my presentations on the topic, I show a slide that captures the essential requirements for fostering this sort of loyalty:

People will not desert a leader; they only desert a boss.
People will not quit a mission; they only quit a job.
People will not leave a team; they only leave an organization.

All Hands on Deck Means No One Goes Overboard

In his book *Profits Aren't Everything, They're the Only Thing* (New York: HarperCollins, 2009), self-proclaimed small-business guru George Cloutier says that business owners should trust no one and micromanage everything; love their business more than their family (and certainly never treat people in the business as a team, much less as a family); keep employees feeling insecure, because "fear is the best motivator"; encourage turnover to continuously shake out the deadwood; and be a "tyrant" who wants people to mindlessly follow orders and not think for themselves. The small-business owners with whom Cloutier consults might make money, but not one of them will ever show up in the Fortune 500, much less make Fortune's lists of the most admired companies or best places to work. And their organizations are unlikely to outlast them. Leaders who build enduringly great organizations take the opposite approach to building relationships.

In this book, you will meet leaders who built great companies that were admired for being successful *and* for being great places to work. Although most of those companies went through a difficult time at some point after the founding leader left, the fact that they all bounced back is a tribute to the culture of ownership that those leaders established. These leaders were human, and each had their flaws and failings. But they all left organizations that have stood the test of time and that have earned incredible loyalty on the part of employees and customers.

This is a work of fiction. The leaders in this book are historical figures, and their companies are very much alive today largely because of the cultural heritage their founding leaders bequeathed. While I have created dialog, I've tried to assure that every line is spoken in the spirit of the leader who is speaking, using actual quotations where possible. The bibliography includes references for learning more about each of these great leaders and more about building a positive corporate culture in general. But if you think you see yourself or someone you know in this book, it is strictly a coincidence. Any errors of omission or commission are mine alone.

All
Hands
On
Deck

1 | Changing "Us and Them" to "We"

For Corey Whitaker, June 13 was the best of times and the worst of times. The week before, he'd been promoted to the CEO position of Owatt Hospitality Services, a Fortune 500 hotel and restaurant enterprise, following an agonizing search process during which he never knew whether he'd be elevated or escorted to the elevator. Yesterday morning, the company's stock price had tanked following an analyst's report that productivity and service-quality problems threatened the very viability of the enterprise. Whitaker had himself only recently become aware of the magnitude of these challenges, since the previous CEO hoarded information like an old pit bull guarding his bone. As executive vice president for marketing, Whitaker was kept out of the loop when it came to operating issues. He smiled and shook his head. The fact that he was out of the loop was undoubtedly why the board had turned the mess over to him.

Whitaker was at the airport, waiting for the sunrise flight from Baltimore to LaGuardia. Later that morning, he had a meeting with the company's bankers, who wanted to know what he was going to do to protect their money. He tried to concentrate on the spreadsheets that just the day before had been loaded onto his laptop but was distracted by the familiar voice of Jack Stallings, business correspondent for CNN, projecting from the television suspended from the ceiling several rows down: "As if the poor economy wasn't already clobbering business travel, tourism, and eating out, it now appears that Owatt Hospitality has shot itself in both feet, with customer satisfaction and revenue per employee both taking big hits in the last quarter."

"You know, we'd solve this economic crisis in about a week if Congress would pass a law saying that these overpaid suits had to get out of their cushy offices; make 'em all get out there on the front lines and do some honest work for a change." Corey hadn't noticed the man when he'd sat down next to him. He was wearing a New York Yankees baseball cap and tinted eyeglasses. Whitaker guessed him to be about 40. He was thin and wiry, with the intense face of a snake eyeing a mouse. "Let 'em get their hands dirty—see what it's like to do some real work for a change."

Whitaker closed up his laptop—he didn't want anyone to see the numerical train wreck represented by that spreadsheet—then self-consciously adjusted his necktie. "I'm sure a lot of those 'suits,' as you call them, would love nothing better than to get out of their offices and not have to deal with bankers, investors, customers, and competitors. Of course, with no 'suit' tending to these things, it wouldn't be long before *nobody* had any 'real work' to do."

The man in the Yankees cap stared hard at Whitaker. "Well, maybe if they'd get out of their offices and talk to people—treat us like adults who might have good ideas and not like children who can't even be trusted to show up on time for work—they might find the ideas they need to fix their businesses have been there all the time, right under their noses. Acres of diamonds and all that, you know." He held out his right hand. "Brent Jacobs. I hope you don't mind me unloading on you like this." Taking a quick look at Whitaker's black pinstripe suit and red silk tie, he added, "And I hope you don't take it personally."

They shook hands. "Not at all. I'll tell you Brent, I'd love to be able to trust people to show up for work because they really wanted to be there, but that's not the real world—at least not where I work. If we didn't have, and enforce, an attendance policy—I shudder to think how people would take advantage of us."

"You say 'us' like the people who work for you are part of 'them' and not part of 'we.' It shouldn't surprise you they don't show up on time." Jacobs crossed his arms, stuck his legs out straight, and glued his stare to the TV.

Whitaker placed the laptop in his briefcase, then looked at his watch. He wanted to dispute Jacobs, to tell him that Owatt Hospitality Services was like a big family where everyone pulled together, where there was no "us" and "them," only "we." But he'd spent the morning looking at employee and customer satisfaction reports, and he knew it wasn't true. When he was in marketing, he and his group had worked on countless annual reports, press releases, and ad campaigns spouting the party line that Owatt's people were partners working together to serve their guests and customers. They were family. And he'd believed it all—or at least had tried hard to believe it. But the black-and-white truth staring up at him from the reports he'd been studying told a different story. Most of Owatt's employees saw themselves as hired hands, not partners—and probably for good reason. The spirit of teamwork he'd enjoyed in the marketing division did not seem to exist in most of the rest of the company.

"So, Brent, you've obviously got some pretty strong opinions about management. What do you do?"

Jacobs kept his eyes fixed on the TV. After a long sigh, he said, "I'm just a bookkeeper. Work nights."

Whitaker cringed inwardly. He hated to hear people describe themselves with the word "just," knowing that in this context, it was often the most unjust word in the English language. "The company I work with has lots of night-shift accountants," he said. "If they don't do their jobs well, we're out of business." He smiled, then added, "Overnight—that's how fast we'd go down the tubes without our 'just' overnight bookkeepers."

"Humph." Jacobs shifted in his chair. "So, where do you work?"

Whitaker laughed softly. "Actually, I work for the company that started this conversation—Owatt Hospitality, the one Jack Stallings was talking about when you sat down."

"No kidding? What do you do there?"

"Well, as of last week, I'm the CEO. According to Stallings, anyway, I've really got my work cut out for me." He looked over at the ticket counter. They were getting ready to board the plane. He squirmed at the prospect that, once they'd boarded and after he'd ensconced himself in the first-class section, Jacobs would walk by and smirk as he headed back to his seat in coach.

"So, you're the new CEO, huh? Should I say congratulations or condolences?"

"I'm not sure. Both, I suppose. So, where do you work, Brent?"

Jacobs stood up and hoisted his backpack. "Surrey Park Inn and Suites in Manhattan. I'm sure you've heard of it."

Whitaker laughed and reached for his briefcase. "Of course I've heard of it." Surrey Park was one of Owatt's premiere properties and one of the few bright spots in the otherwise dismal portrait of a company that, according to Jack Stallings, was headed for Niagara Falls in a barrel.

Over the loudspeaker came the announcement, "We are now seating our first-class passengers, plus anyone else who needs a little extra time going down the jetway." A very frequent flyer, Whitaker boarded through this gate regularly. The woman now standing behind the counter was always cheerful and helpful. He made a mental note to give her a business card—once the new ones were printed up. She would, he thought to himself, make a great member of the Owatt team—once they were back in hiring mode, anyway.

After he'd boarded, Whitaker didn't notice whether Jacobs smirked as he walked through the first-class section; he was again absorbed in his spreadsheets. And he was already heading for the limo stand by the time Jacobs deplaned. He made another mental note to stay at the Surrey Park Inn and Suites the next time he was in town and to look up Brent Jacobs in the back office on the night shift.

There was a man in a tuxedo standing just outside the security gate with Whitaker's name on a placard. "Have you got any luggage, sir?" he asked after Whitaker introduced himself.

"Not the kind you can see," Whitaker replied with a smile. "Just a quick in-and-out today."

"Well, let me take that for you, anyway," the chauffeur said, reaching for Whitaker's briefcase. "My name's Jeff Saunders." He pointed toward the revolving door. "We're right out here."

Through the revolving door, Whitaker saw a black stretch limo with smoked-glass windows. It gleamed like it had just come off the factory line. "The other guest arrived a bit early. He's already in the car waiting for us."

"Other guest?" Whitaker tried to hide his displeasure at the news he'd be sharing his limo with someone else. He'd planned to use the drive for final preparation and had no time for or interest in bantering with another stranger.

"Yes, sir. It's Mr. Disney. He said you'd know him."

Whitaker shook his head. Of course, Owatt had properties near every Disney theme park but as far as he knew had never dealt directly with anyone from the Disney family. For that matter, he didn't even know if there were any living members of the family still around.

"Should I put your briefcase in the trunk, or would you like to hang on to it?"

"I'll hang on to it, thanks."

Saunders opened the back door and set the briefcase on the floor next to the side-facing seat. Whitaker saw penny loafers and the lower legs of a pair of white slacks as he stooped to get into the limo. With one foot on the floor of the car and one foot on the curb, he froze in place. He'd seen the man in the seat opposite him before—the man with the thin mustache and the big smile. As a child, he'd seen him every Saturday morning on television.

"Mr. Whitaker, meet Mr. Disney," Saunders said as he held the door.

The man with the mustache smiled and touched his forehead in a casual salute. "Please, it's Walt. A pleasure to meet you. Have a seat, Corey. We've got a lot to do and not much time to do it."

2 | Real Ownership Is of the Heart, Not of the Wallet

Corey hardly noticed the airport terminal fade into the distance through the limo's smoked-glass window. He just stared at the man who had been introduced as Walt Disney. After a very long moment, his eyes narrowed, and he allowed the slightest smile to crease his mouth. "That was very good, Mr.—uhm—Mr. Disney, did you say?"

"That's right. And I'm sure this must all be quite disorienting for you."

"Disorienting? Oh no, not at all—once I figured out your game."

"My game?" Disney smiled wryly. "And just what do you think my game is, Corey?"

Corey leaned back in his seat and shook his head with a laugh. "As the guy who plans meetings and conferences for one of the world's largest hospitality companies, I get sales pitches from you motivational look-alikes all the time. The Ben Franklin look-alike sends me a key and a kite and tells me he will electrify my organization. The Teddy Roosevelt look-alike tells me he'll fire up the troops to charge the hill. The Dirty Harry look-alike tells me he'll make my day. But for a Walt Disney look-alike to hijack my cab ... I have to hand it to you, bud, you really do have chutzpah. So, where are you taking me, 'Mr. Disney'—to the Magic Kingdom?"

Disney didn't answer but tapped the window that separated the two men from the driver's compartment. The window slid open. "Yes, Mr. Disney?"

"Jeff, Corey wants to go to the Magic Kingdom. Can we fit that in and still get him to his meeting on time?"

"No problem, Mr. Disney." The window whispered shut, and Corey felt the limo accelerate.

Corey shook his head. "No, 'Walt,' there is a problem. This game's gone far enough, whatever your name is. It's not funny anymore. Now we're talking kidnapping, and you could get twenty years in the federal pen. You had better—"

"Ah, *Kidnapped*," Disney said with a heartfelt sigh. "The great Robert Louis Stevenson classic. I'd always wanted to make that movie. There's just never enough time, is there, Corey?"

Before he could reply, Corey felt the car slow down and come to a stop. He knew they hadn't been driving long enough to have reached the bank building and was about to protest when the side door opened and a burst of frigid air shot into the passenger cabin. "We're here," Disney said, tapping Corey on the knee as he scooted across and stepped out of the limo. "You can leave your briefcase in the car."

Corey looked out the door, blinked hard, and shook his head. Then he looked out again. It was snowing hard—in July. "We need to get moving if you're going to get to your meeting on time," Disney said, motioning Corey to get out of the limo.

Corey swung himself around and stepped outside—and into another world. It couldn't have been much more than 10 degrees outside, and snowflakes were flying past horizontally on a driving wind. Disney tugged on Corey's sleeve. "Come on, let's go before you freeze to death."

"What the ... What's going on?" Corey stepped gingerly into the snow, following Disney's lead.

"You'll understand soon enough, Corey. For now, just follow me. And pay attention. You'll never see this again." Disney led Corey through the snow toward a small hill. Over the top, Corey found himself looking into a painting he'd seen in history books. Only this time, the picture wasn't in a frame. And the figures were moving. He couldn't hear anything over the wind, but he knew he was watching one of the most famous and pivotal scenes in American history being played out—seemingly in real life. A man he immediately recognized as George Washington was speaking to a small group of patriots at Valley Forge. The men were sitting on tree stumps, stooped and sullen, and even from this remove, Corey could tell that whatever Washington was telling them, he had a hard sell to make.

Disney put a hand on Corey's shoulder. Spellbound, he'd forgotten his shock and the cold as he'd watched the father of the country imploring his tatterdemalion troops. "You know what he's saying?" Disney asked, and without waiting for an answer, continued: "He's telling those men that he can't pay them, he can't feed or supply them, he can't safeguard their lives, and he can't guarantee their ultimate success; and still, he wants them to stay with him, starving and freezing, to fight for their country—a country that does not yet exist except in the dreams of men like this. You know why I'm showing you this, Corey?"

Corey shook his head as he hugged his shoulders. He was shivering so badly that he couldn't have spoken even if he knew the answer.

"I brought you here because this is a great metaphor for the challenge that you're going to face in your company. These men—the men to whom you and your countrymen owe your freedom—had a sense of ownership that transcended paychecks, stock options, perks, and benefits. That spirit of ownership underlies every great organization. And that will be your challenge, young man: to build a culture of ownership. It's going to be an arduous journey. Are you up for the challenge?"

George Washington was now down on one knee, eye to eye with his men. He was still speaking earnestly, holding one fist to his chest. The men were nodding grudging affirmations.

Corey felt tears on his cheeks and his heart in his throat. "I don't know."

"That's good, Corey. I'd worry if you weren't filled with doubt and concern. But shall we start the journey, anyway?"

Corey nodded, and just like that, a small vehicle appeared in front of the two men, like one of the cars you would see on a ride at a Disney theme park. Walt nudged Corey into the seat and the car started moving, leaving the snows of Valley Forge behind.

Over the next several minutes, Corey saw American history play out right in front of him—a panorama of covered wagons, farmers, inventors, factories, burgeoning cities, and highways unfolding themselves across the landscape. After a while, Walt spoke. "What drove all these people—the men and women who made this country great? It wasn't just the desire for money and material things. They wanted to be part of something bigger than themselves. They wanted to own something—something more than just stuff. To this day, it's that spirit of ownership that galvanizes every great organization and motivates the people who make those organizations great."

The ride—for that's what Corey had decided they were on—came to a stop at an old-fashioned blacksmith shop, with animatronics as real as he'd ever seen in any theme park. The man inside, who could not have been more lifelike, was pounding a horseshoe on an anvil. He picked it up with his tongs, inspected it carefully, then placed it back on the anvil and resumed pounding—a process he repeated several times before Disney spoke again. "You see the pride he's putting into that horseshoe? That's ownership. He does not own the shop; he's renting the space. But he owns something far more important. He owns his work. He's an owner in the ways that matter most. You see, real ownership is of the heart, not of the wallet."

Corey shook his head in disagreement. "That might have been true in this man's day"—he nodded toward the blacksmith, who'd just dunked the glowing horseshoe into a bucket of water and was now inspecting it again—"assuming he's not just an idealized and nostalgic representation of 'the good old days,' and assuming they really were that good, but in today's world, people don't buy in; they have to be bought in. If I tried to hire a new executive team member—say, someone to replace me in the senior marketing role—without an offer of stock options, they'd laugh in my face."

Corey didn't see Disney push any buttons, but the car was suddenly moving again. A moment later, they stopped in front of another exhibit—this time, a modern executive office with plate-glass windows on two sides overlooking busy city streets below. The occupant was leaned back in a plush leather chair with his feet propped up on an obviously expensive desk, speaking into his cell phone. The plaque on his desk announced to the world that he was Jerrold P. Winters, Executive Vice President. The smile on his face suggested that he'd just won the lottery. "That's right, babe. Stock price hit eighty today. My options are locked in, and we can cash out. So, think about where you want to live, because we can go anywhere. I've got headhunters calling me all day long." He laughed as he disconnected the call.

"Mr. Jerrold P. Winters was hired by Intellikey Corporation four years ago," Disney said, "with a stated mission of wringing cost out of this organization. He's been very good at it. More than a thousand people—about a quarter of the company's workforce—have gotten pink slips. Today, Jerrold locked in an eight-figure stock option. This time next year, he'll have moved up the food chain to be CEO of some other company whose board mistakenly thinks they need a chainsaw when what they really need is fertilizer."

Jerrold P. Winters stood up and adjusted his suit coat. Leaving his briefcase on the credenza as he passed by, he strolled to the door, whistling a happy tune. "Let's go down a few levels," Disney said, and with no more warning than that, he and Corey were plunged into darkness. Corey had the sensation of being trapped in a falling elevator. Just as suddenly, the ride slowed to a stop in front of a large office space filled with cubicles, only one of which was occupied. "Ralph Marten has been with Intellikey about as long as Jerrold P. Winters has—except he doesn't have any stock options. He's here at nine-thirty this evening rather than being home with his family because several months ago, he was told he had to fire six people from his twenty-person department. Tonight, he ate dinner at his desk while he tried to catch up on the work those six other people used to do. And you know what he's doing now? He's working on a reference letter for one of the people he had to fire. He wants it to be perfect; it's a real act of love. He'll be here till midnight, writing and rewriting."

Corey looked more closely at the cubicle farm Ralph Marten inhabited. Indeed, it looked like every fourth one had been stripped bare. It reminded Corey of a blighted urban neighborhood where windows were boarded over. Marten ripped the top page from the yellow pad he'd been working on, wadded it into a tight ball, and threw it at the trash can across the room, missing by a good eight feet. Then he planted his forehead on his hands and screamed.

Disney was visibly sad as he looked from Ralph Marten to Corey. "The real question isn't what you're going to tell your board, is it? It's what you're going to tell people like Ralph Marten." Corey knew that the primary agenda item at next month's Owatt board meeting would be cost cutting and that a number of his board members expected his first act as CEO would be to eliminate jobs. He had to choose between that and selling off assets, and of course, the money-making assets would be the most marketable.

He thought he could get an asset sale through his board, but it would be a fight. Layoffs would be a much easier sale.

The ride started up again, now traveling through a velvet twilight. "So, Corey, tell me: Who's the *real* owner at Intellikey? Is it the guy who's going home to update his resume and take his wife out to a fancy restaurant because he just came into a wheelbarrow full of stock certificates, or is it the guy who's sitting at his desk with vending-machine food, writing reference letters because he still feels the burden of loyalty to people who don't even work for the company anymore? Which one really owns the work, and which one is just renting a spot on the organization chart?"

They rode in silence for a while before Disney spoke again. "When the board interviewed you for the CEO position, you told them you wanted to build a culture of ownership." By this time, it didn't even occur to Corey to wonder how Disney knew what had transpired in his job interview. "What sort of a culture of ownership were you talking about, Corey? The type you buy or the type you earn?"

Corey looked down at his hands, still tightly clenched about the grab bar of the ride. "The type you earn," he replied, wishing that his voice had carried more conviction.

"If you're serious about that, it's a much tougher row to hoe than just trying to buy it. Are you serious about it?"

Corey thought back on his conversation with Brent Jacobs earlier that morning in the airport. *I hope you're not going to be just another empty suit who cares more about dollars than he does about real people.* Corey had been insulted when Jacobs said it, but now he realized that was exactly what some members of his board—and virtually every trader on Wall Street—expected him to be: another suit who cared more about the bottom line than about his employees. "Dead serious," he replied, and this time there was a lot more conviction behind the words.

"You're going to need help," Disney said. Corey nodded, and Disney continued. "You're going to have to change some of the ways you think about business, and about people."

"I know you're right, Walt, but it's pretty ironic. The board hired me because of what they think I already know about business and people." Corey shot a quick glance at his fellow passenger and was surprised at not being surprised that he was now on a first-name basis with one of history's most beloved business leaders—a man who had been dead for nearly half a century.

"What will be even harder, Corey, is that you are also going to have to change yourself. Have you read the book Sarah Kieley gave you?" Kieley was the executive recruiter the board had retained for the CEO search.

"You mean *What Got You Here Won't Get You There* by—what's his name? Marshall Goldsmith?"

"That one. As Goldsmith says, being a hard-charging, goal-achieving manager got you here, but it won't get you where you want to go from this point on. Let's go meet some of the people who can help you get from here to there. But first, I'm starving! Let's go get a hot dog."

Corey shook his head. "Walt, I'd love a hot dog, but we've really got to get back. I'm sure I'm already late for my meeting at the bank."

"Nah, don't worry about that. We'll grab a hot dog, meet the people you need to meet, and Jeff will still get you back to the bank in plenty of time for your meeting."

Corey laughed. "Walt, there's no way we can pack all of that in and still get me to the bank on time. That would take a real magic act."

"Yes, it would," Disney replied with a knowing smile. "And I am the king of the Magic Kingdom."

3 | Lesson 1: Start with a Mission that is Bigger Than the Business

Corey and Walt were seated at a picnic table, eating their hot dogs. A cheerful tune floated on the air, and Corey had the vague sense that throngs of people were nearby, though he couldn't see past the fog that hovered all around the two men. When he'd finished his hot dog, Walt leaned forward on his elbows and gave Corey a hard stare. "How much do you know about business history?" Walt raised his eyebrows in the manner of a teacher who clearly expected that his student would have done his homework.

"Well, I haven't made a formal study of it or anything like that, but I know enough, I suppose."

"You know enough, you suppose?"

"Okay, there's a lot more I could learn. But I'm much more interested in the here and now, and what the future can bring, than I am the past. Water that's gone over the dam never goes back into the reservoir." Corey smiled, pleased with his clever metaphor, and hoped that Walt would catch its meaning.

"The deepest water never goes over the dam at all," Walt replied. "There is great wisdom in the depths of the past. In fact, you can learn most everything you need to know about building a great organization by studying strategies that were used by leaders who have already done it."

"Or the ones who are doing it now."

"The ones who are doing it now learned from the ones who have already done it, I assure you. Tell me, Corey: What one product, more than any other, defined and shaped the first half of the twentieth century?"

Corey thought for a moment, then replied, "The automobile?"

"Absolutely. Everything about America and the modern world has been influenced by the automobile: where we live, what we do,

21

how we spend our time and money—indeed, the very way we see ourselves. And what company transformed the automobile from being an odd novelty to being the central driver of our culture, economy, and society?"

"Uhm, I'd say Ford Motor Company and the Model T."

"Yes, I'd say so. And who was the leader who built the Ford Motor Company?"

"Henry Ford. Everyone knows that."

"Okay. Passing marks so far. What product, more than any other, shaped and defined the second half of the twentieth century?"

When Corey thought for a few seconds longer than Walt's patience would tolerate, he said, "This one should be easy for you."

"The computer?"

"Of course. It's almost impossible to imagine your world without the computer, isn't it? And what company towered above everyone else in the computer industry?"

"That would be IBM."

Walt nodded. "And who was the leader who built IBM?"

"Thomas Watson—both of them, Senior and Junior."

"That's right. When Tom Watson Senior changed the name of the Computing-Recording-Tabulating Company to International Business Machines in 1924, it had about three thousand employees and eleven million dollars in sales. When he finally handed the reins over to Tom Junior, the company had something like seventy thousand employees and sales of almost one billion dollars. He gave his son a terrific platform upon which to build an even greater company. Now, let's look at more recent history. What sort of experience have those two companies had over the past decade or so?"

Corey rubbed his chin. "Well, IBM nearly went under. I remember being in management meetings where we discussed the dire impact on our company if IBM were to go belly-up. And Ford nearly collapsed with the rest of its domestic auto industry a few years ago."

"And where are they both now?"

"Hmm. IBM seems to be doing great. As I recall, they made a big move from mainly selling and servicing equipment to also providing consulting solutions."

"That's right. And in doing that, they were really going back to the spirit of innovation and entrepreneurship that Tom Watson built into the company. But they did something even more important. They remembered the key insight upon which the elder Watson founded his entire business strategy—something that no one else had ever done before, and something that has been a model for every great company since. Watson recognized that corporate culture could be a powerful and sustained source of competitive advantage. More than any other factor, the company's culture was the driving force behind its growth during the good times and its resilience during the bad times—including the Great Depression."

Corey looked down at his hands folded on the table for a few seconds, deep in thought, then looked back up at Walt. "It's sort of a paradox, when you think about it. I mean, here you have IBM, in the most left-brain of all industries—data processing—using corporate culture, the most right-brain of all business strategies, to dominate the market."

"Yep," Walt replied. "Watson intuitively grasped something that all great business leaders know: You need both left- and right-brain qualities. You need left-brain management to count the beans, but it's the creative power of right-brain leadership that plants those beans in the first place. Lewis Gerstner was the man IBM brought in as CEO when it appeared the company was about to go over a cliff. He later wrote a book about the experience—*Who Says Elephants Can't Dance?* Have you read it?"

Corey shook his head as he pulled a pen and note card from his coat pocket and wrote down the title. "No, but I will."

"You should. One of the most important things Gerstner did was tap into the cultural heritage of the historical IBM. In fact, in his book he said that he came to realize culture wasn't just part of the game; culture was the *entire* game. In other words, he knew that the future of IBM would be won or lost by their success or failure at reconnecting with the culture and the traditions of the past."

Corey made another note on his card.

"What about Ford?" Walt asked when Corey had finished writing.

"Well, I don't follow the auto industry as well as I should"—Corey laughed when Walt raised an eyebrow—"or as well as I'm going to starting right now! But I do know that when the domestic auto industry went into the dumpster, Ford was the only one of the Big Three that avoided bankruptcy. And from what I've read, they still seem to be doing pretty well compared to the rest of the Motor City."

"Would you like to see how it all started, this culture of ownership that powers growth in good times and sustains survival in bad times?"

"Sure."

"Come on, then; let's go for a ride." Walt got up, and Corey followed him into the mist. After a few steps, they came upon a Ford Mustang convertible, only it was unlike any Mustang Corey had ever seen. There was no steering wheel or center console, no chrome exhaust pipes, no dials or gauges on the dashboard, no buttons or switches on the doors. The four bucket seats looked like they belonged in a conference room rather than a car. A commanding voice emanated from the car. "Walt! Corey! If you guys moved any slower, you'd fall over. If all you want is a slow Sunday cruise, call up a Camaro. Otherwise, let's get a move on. I've got two thousand wild horses that aren't going to stay in the stable much longer."

Corey looked over at Walt. "A car with a sense of humor? And he can't possibly mean he's got two thousand horsepower under that hood." Walt just smiled. The doors snapped open, and the two front seats swiveled around in an obvious invitation for Walt and Corey to climb on board. A jet-engine-like roar blasted their ear drums as if in answer to the way Corey had questioned the Mustang's manhood. He laughed at how he was mentally anthropomorphizing the modernistic machine into an impatient teenager gunning the engine.

Walt motioned Corey into the seat on the right and took the other one himself. The seats swiveled back into the car, and the doors closed with a solid click. A four-point harness system clasped itself around each passenger, so gently that Corey hardly even noticed it. "This is amazing," he said as he watched a computer display panel count down the seconds to launch.

"The best minds of Ford and IBM, working together ten years in your future. Get ready for the ride of your life, Corey."

Just like that, Corey was pressed back into the seat as the Mustang rocketed off through space and time. "How does it know where to go?" Corey shouted over at Walt, and then he realized that the ride was so quiet, he could have just whispered.

"Instinct," Walt replied. "Like a giant sea turtle returns to the place of its birth, this Mustang is taking us to the time and place he was born. There's something there you need to see." The Mustang glided to a stop in front of a giant blue velvet curtain, and the car tilted forward slightly to give the men a better view. There was a moment of intense anticipation, and then the curtain drew back. Corey was looking down upon what was obviously a primitive assembly-line floor. From the clothes the men wore and the tools they were working with, he guessed the year to be 1900 or so. A man in an old-fashioned business suit was walking the floor, stopping to talk to people along the way.

"That's Henry Ford," Walt said. "Watch this." Ford stopped at a work station where a man was obviously struggling to figure out how to use one of his tools. Ford tapped him on the shoulder, took the wrench from him, and showed him what to do with it. He repeated the action several times, then watched the other man do it until he got it right. Oblivious to the grime on the man's shirt and the grease on his own hands, Ford put his arm around the worker's shoulder and gave him some obvious words of encouragement.

Just then, another worker walked down the line and gave Ford a playful punch in the arm. Still dressed in his suit jacket, Ford tackled the man, and they fell on the shop floor in a wrestling match. The other men gathered about, cheering them on. After a few minutes, it was obvious the match would end in a draw. The two men separated, breathing heavily and laughing heartily. Then, with an expression of mock anger on his face, Ford waved both arms, motioning his men to get back to work. He rubbed his hands on a dirty rag, straightened his suit coat, and walked out of the picture. The curtain closed on the stage.

"You've just seen young Henry Ford—a Henry Ford not many people remember, but one who created a culture of ownership that was strong enough to help the company survive and thrive, even as this young leader morphed into the dictator we more commonly associate with his name. The men you just saw would have done anything for Henry, and over time, that allegiance attached itself to the Ford Motor Company. That will be a consistent theme in our travels: A culture of ownership almost always begins with personal loyalty—and that is always a two-way street. Let's watch the second act."

The curtain reopened. A man who was more recognizably Henry Ford of the history books was standing behind a podium, speaking to a room full of men who, it quickly became apparent, were newspaper reporters. "The year is 1914," Walt said, "and you are watching one of the most astonishing press conferences ever called by a corporation. Henry Ford has just announced that Ford Motor Company is reducing the workday from nine hours to eight hours and at the same time is *doubling* the daily wage of its workers to five dollars. The Five Dollar Day, as it came to be called, was going to cost Ford ten million dollars. That was big money back then," he added with an impish grin.

"I remember reading about that in school," Corey said. "He raised wages so his people could afford to buy his cars—turned out to be a pretty good business decision."

"Yes, it was. But it was more than that. Remember I said that a culture of ownership is not a matter of wallet—it's a matter of heart. That's as true for people in the corner office as it is for people in the cubicles. You cannot command loyalty; you have to earn it. Let's listen in for a minute."

Corey suddenly heard the jostling of reporters competing for attention. The man standing just to Ford's left, presumably one of his lieutenants, pointed to a face in the crowd. "Mr. Ford, you already dominate the car business, and you've had no trouble recruiting enough men to work in your factory. Shouldn't this money have gone to the shareholders as a return on their capital and not to the hired hands, who are lucky to have a job anyway?"

"Yeah," shouted a reporter from the other end of the room, "ain't this just more red socialism dressed up in a business suit?" The comment set off a wave of murmurs throughout the room.

Ford motioned for quiet. "This plan has nothing to do with any 'ism' whatever. Our company is making money enough to run our business and to do more good in the world, and I'm glad to do it."

Ford raised both arms to silence another round of murmuring. "Look, you fellows out there need to understand that the success of our company does not just belong to me and the other people who happen to own stock. It also belongs to the people whose work has made it possible. Any man who works in a factory deserves sufficient wages to keep him out of debt, to keep him in comfort, to give him a good home, and to educate his children."

Another round of murmurs percolated through the room, only this time they seemed more supportive of Ford's comments. "That's right" and "That's the truth" were among the comments Corey heard the reporters mutter.

Ford continued. "Factory owners must realize that their workers are human like themselves and should be treated humanely, same as they'd want to be treated or have members of their own families treated. We believe that doing the right thing for our people is also the right thing for our business, and . . ."

The curtain closed, cutting off Ford's final words. Corey felt the Mustang power up again. As they flew along—and Corey did indeed have the sensation of great speed—Walt grinned like a teenager out for his first joy ride. "We have one more stop to make," he said. The Mustang pulled to a stop in front of what looked like a giant drive-in theater screen. "This is happening right now." The screen came to life, but the images were all in 3-D; Corey felt like he could have stepped out of the car and walked right into the meeting being played out in front of them.

There were about 30 people in the room, men and women, dressed mostly in conservative business attire. "These people are all descendants of Henry Ford," Walt said. "They meet every three months, something they've done for more than twenty years. If you see concern written on their faces, it's because they are collectively the largest holders of Ford Motor Company stock—and the value of that stock is currently less than ten percent of what it once was.

On top of that, they've lost tens of millions of dollars in forgone dividends. Today they've decided—once more—to stand behind their company, even though short term, they could probably make a lot more money by selling their Ford stock and investing it elsewhere."

As the picture on the screen began to fade away, Corey heard one of the people in the room speaking: "*Investors* just own stock certificates—pieces of paper—and paper is easy to walk away from. But we're *owners* of this organization, not just paper investors, and ownership comes with a responsibility to the people of that organization—employees and customers as well as shareholders. It's not just about money; it's about engagement, commitment, and pride. As owners, we need to stand by our company and stand by our people."

The screen went blank, and the Mustang pulled away. "The scenes you've just seen were separated by more than one hundred years," Walt said. "Especially in his later years, there was a lot to not like about Henry Ford, but that culture of ownership he created in the early years was largely responsible for assuring that Ford Motor Company would survive him, even when he was at his worst. Like all great leaders, Henry Ford framed the mission of his company in terms of changing the world. He wasn't just selling cars; he was changing the way we live and work. He wasn't just running factories; he was making life better for the people who worked there. It's the same today. Steve Jobs didn't frame Apple's mission as selling computers but rather as transforming the way we learn, work, and interact with each other. Bill McGowan wasn't selling phones at MCI; he was trying to break the AT&T monopoly that for too long had stifled innovation and provided mediocre and overpriced services. Herb Kelleher didn't just start another airline; he created a whole new model for building a business."

Walt looked hard at Corey, checking to see that he was taking all this in. "Organizations that are 'built to last,' to quote the title of a book I'm sure you've read, all have a culture of own-ership, one way or another. People like Jerrold P. Winters—who are just high-priced hired hands temporarily renting corner offices until something better comes along—are eventually rejected by the organization's culture in the way a body will reject a mismatched organ. That's what happened to Carly Fiorina at Hewlett-Packard and Robert Nardelli at Home Depot. They were rejected by the culture of the organizations they were hired to run because their values, beliefs, and goals were so antagonistic to the historic culture. That will be your paramount challenge at Owatt, Corey: building a culture of ownership where people think and act like partners in the enterprise, not just investors in the business or hired hands in the operation."

Corey felt the Mustang slowing down again. "Well, look here," Walt exclaimed with delight. The Mustang came to a stop next to a sidewalk vendor selling ice-cream cones. The door opened, and the two men stepped out. "Chocolate or vanilla?" Walt asked while reaching for his wallet.

"I really don't have time," Corey said as he looked at his watch. It read 7:11 in the morning—the same time it had been when he stepped into the limo at the airport. *The best way to escape the rapids is to flow with the white water, not to fight against it.* Over the years, Corey had realized that many of the things he'd learned on his first Outward Bound expedition applied to life in general. In the back of his mind, he could sense the voice of his instructor telling him that this was one of those times to just flow with it. He closed his eyes, took a slow deep breath, then looked back at his watch. It still read 7:11. "I'll have chocolate," he said with a resigned smile.

4 | Lesson 2: Use Structure and Process to Create Culture

Walt and Corey walked in silence for a while as they finished their ice-cream cones. Corey had the sensation that they were passing by other features in Walt's ethereal theme park, though he couldn't see them. In the distance, he heard what sounded like a men's choir, though the closer they came, the more obvious it was that many of the voices were off-key. Walt brushed the last bits of waffle cone from his fingers. "Winston Churchill said that we first shape our buildings, and then our buildings shape us. When we designed buildings for the Magic Kingdom, we wanted people to experience the happiest place on earth. I knew the experience would begin with the physical structures, but that would only be the beginning of the experience. Though I didn't use the term 'cultural blueprinting' at the time, I always knew we had to put as much thought into the invisible architecture as we did the architecture that can be seen with the eyes."

"Invisible architecture?" Just as Corey finished his ice-cream cone and wadded up the napkin, they happened by a wastebasket.

"Yes. Invisible architecture is made up of the values, the culture, and the emotional feel of an organization. It is ultimately more important than the physical buildings in determining how engaged people are in their work, which of course profoundly affects how well customers enjoy their experience." They were getting closer to the sound of the singing voices, and it was more clearly obvious that this was a bunch of amateurs belting out a song. The tune was vaguely familiar, but Corey couldn't make out the words.

"Most business leaders intuitively know that the invisible dimension of their organization is important," Walt continued, "but they rarely put the same care and effort into creating a cultural blueprint that they put into the physical design of their factories,

33

offices, and showrooms. The first person who really understood this, and acted upon it, was Tom Watson. From the day he started with the company you know as IBM, Watson paid excruciating attention to the details of his corporate culture. Under his leadership, and later that of Tom Junior, IBM's culture of ownership became a formidable source of competitive advantage. Would you like to see how he did it?"

"Sure," Corey replied.

"Watch your step," Walt said as he grabbed Corey by the elbow and guided him down a set of stairs and into what appeared to be a row of theater seats. The men in the choir had just launched into a new song. Though Corey still couldn't see them, he could now make out the words as they sang:

There's a feeling everywhere of bigger things in store,
Of new horizons coming into view.

"Let's sit here," Walt whispered as though trying to not disturb other moviegoers that Corey could not see. The men kept on singing:

The will to win is built right in,
It will not be denied.
And we will go ahead we know,
By working side by side.

As Corey took his seat, the curtain opened on a stage below. About 30 men in dark suits and white shirts were singing in unison. What they lacked in talent, they made up for with enthusiasm. With their double-breasted jackets and slicked-back hair, they looked like a gang of extras in a Depression-era movie.

Ever onward, ever onward,
That's the Spirit that has brought us fame.

Walt leaned over and whispered, "These are IBM salesmen. They're singing the IBM fight song. It was one of Watson's favorites."

"You're kidding, right? These are salesmen? And they're singing the—the IBM fight song?"

We're big but bigger we will be.
We can't fail for all to see,
That to serve humanity
Has been our aim.

"Yes. It's one of the songs in the IBM songbook."

"I can't believe it. There's actually an IBM songbook? And the salespeople actually sing together?"

"Salesmen. Back then, they were all men. And yes, they did sing IBM fight songs. It might seem ridiculous today."

"Now there's an understatement," Corey said under his breath as he imagined himself trying to lead a chorus of Owatt employees in a company fight song.

"It probably seemed silly to some IBMers even back then. But it didn't seem silly to any of these guys." The men on the stage were shuffling through their songbooks, obviously looking for the next tune.

"Who are they?"

"That's the IBM Hundred Percent Club, class of 1936. At a time when more than one-quarter of American workers were unemployed, these guys were taking home a decent paycheck. But more than that, at a time when there was so much cynicism in the land, they really believed the words in those songs. There was a sense of destiny: They were going to win and continue to grow. They really did believe they were part of an enterprise making a better world—that they really were serving humanity. And they really were proud to be a part of a great company."

"What's the Hundred Percent Club?" As the lights slowly dimmed, Corey could see the stage rotating clockwise as the curtain closed in front of it.

"The Hundred Percent Club was for salespeople who met or exceeded one hundred percent of their sales quotas. It was a big deal. You might think these songs are silly, but the spirit of those singers delighted customers and terrified competitors." The curtain had now closed completely, and the room was pitch black. "Hang on," Walt said, "this is really good."

Suddenly and without warning, Corey's ears were blasted by the shrieking of a train whistle, followed by an explosive crash that rocked the seats like an earthquake. A cacophony of screams rolled across the unseen audience. The curtain slowly opened, and the singing salesmen had been replaced by a train wreck. It appeared that one train had collided with another, hitting it from behind. Several train cars were lying on their sides, a cloud of acrid smoke slowly spread over the scene, and the final rumblings of the crash were now giving way to screams of pain and cries for help.

"Port Jervis, New York, 1924." Walt was again whispering as one might do in a movie theater. "It was IBM Day at the World's Fair, and Tom Watson had commissioned trains to bring in his employees to enjoy the festivities. At Port Jervis, one of the trains slowed suddenly, and the one behind it couldn't stop in time. No one was killed, but more than a hundred were injured, many seriously."

"Man," Corey exclaimed, "I bet that ruined IBM Day at the fair!"

"Quite to the contrary," Walt replied. "Old Man Watson turned what could have been a real tragedy—not to mention a public relations black eye—into an opportunity to show the IBM culture at its best, and in the process, to gain the sort of advertising that you simply cannot buy."

"How'd he do it?"

"Watch." The stage was again rotating. A man Corey presumed to be Tom Watson was barking orders to his assistants. "Baumwell, I want you to call Dr. Smith down at the hospital. Tell him to round up as many medical men as he can find and that you'll get them all to Port Jervis. I want them there by dinnertime. Smith, you make sure everyone who was hurt gets a bouquet of flowers. And not just daffodils—make it roses. Nichols, you type up a letter for my signature, telling each person how much we appreciate them and that they are not to worry about their medical expenses. We will provide for that. Carlson, I want you to . . . ."

Watson's voice faded away as the stage rotated once more. Now they were looking inside a hospital ward of the old-fashioned type. Tom Watson and a woman Corey presumed to be his wife were working their way down the ward, stopping at every bed to visit each patient. There was a vase full of roses at every bedside. Walt again whispered: "Tom Watson could be real tough to work for. So could Tom Junior. But he was also compassionate and generous, which was one reason why so many IBM people were so loyal. A big part of his genius was the ability to transform seemingly insignificant, or even adverse, happenings into vehicles to help define the company's culture—to help make the statement 'We're IBM, and this is our way of doing things.' Many little stories like this were woven together to help tell—and sell—IBM's big story."

The stage finished its rotation, and they were now looking down on a classroom filled with young people wearing business suits. There was a calendar on the wall, and Corey made out the year 1946. At the front of the room, an older man—clearly the instructor—was writing on a blackboard. Above the blackboard was an engraved wooden sign that simply read:

THINK

"This was one of Watson's most powerful culture-building tools," Walt said. "The IBM school. Every new salesperson went through it—and I say salesperson now because by this time, IBM was one of the first companies to open opportunities for women—and later for minorities. Of course, the new people were taught selling skills. How could it have been otherwise, since Tom Watson was one of the greatest salesmen ever born? And they learned about the products they would be selling. But the IBM school was a lot more. It was where new people learned about the company's values and culture and what was expected of them. By the time they graduated, they had a very good idea of whether they were going to make it with the company. And for most people who decided they wanted to make it, they generally made it for a long time."

Corey nodded appreciatively. "I would like to learn more about Watson's approach to building a corporate culture like that, if for no other reason than that employee turnover costs my company millions of dollars a year. And that's just the direct cost of recruiting and training new people. The indirect cost of inefficiency and poor customer service caused by inexperienced staff adds millions of dollars more to that figure."

"There's another cost beyond the ones you've just mentioned that most companies don't account for," Walt said, "but it's a very real cost and might even be a bigger problem."

"What cost is that, Walt?"

"The cost of hiring people who don't really fit with your culture and then, in many cases, firing them once the misfit becomes too painfully obvious. The computer engineer who is happy as a clam at Apple might be miserable working at IBM, and vice versa, even though the job descriptions are the same. That's one reason why it's so important to have a cultural blueprint. If you don't know who you are as an organization, you're much more likely to hire people who don't fit. It's a disservice to them, and it's a disservice to the people they're going to have to work with, at least until they quit or get terminated."

Corey pulled another note card from his pocket. "We've been talking about corporate culture all morning—at least I think it's still morning. It occurs to me that for all I've heard, read, and spoken about the topic, I've never really defined it. What's your take on it, Walt?"

"Well, there's the textbook definition, which is that culture is the fabric of an organization's values, beliefs, philosophies, practices, traditions, customs, and rituals. But I tend to think of it in simpler terms: Culture is to the organization what personality and character are to the individual. Southwest Airlines and United Airlines are in the same business, but in terms of corporate culture, they are on different planets."

Corey made another note, then said, "You used the term 'cultural blueprint' a minute ago. Do you really create a blueprint, like what you would put together to design a new building?"

"Well," Walt replied, "when you consider that the invisible architecture of values and culture has a greater impact on the experience of workers and customers alike than the physical architecture does, don't you think it would be a good idea? At Disney, I never drew up a cultural blueprint on paper, though I probably should have, but I did have a very clear blueprint in my mind. And this mental blueprint guided everything we did, from recruiting and orientation to training and performance evaluation. Like Tom Watson at IBM, I made sure that every structure and every process at Disney was developed to create a unique culture. I think we were pretty successful at that."

Corey nodded. "There's another masterful understatement!" After making a few more notes, he said, "This all makes a lot of sense, but I don't think I've ever read a book or even an article that describes a process for creating a cultural blueprint. Have you ever seen anything like that?"

"Nope, can't say that I have. Watching you take notes just now, I'm assuming that's what you're going to do. You know, I was always so busy on the creative side of the business that I never really had the chance to sit down and write a book about my ideas on business leadership. It was something I always wanted to do someday but never quite got around to." He smiled and poked Corey on the arm. "There's never going to be enough time, so keep writing. That's a book the world needs right now, and it would be great advertising for Owatt Hospitality. You don't think this little adventure is just for you, do you? You need to teach and you need to write; you need to share what you've learned with others, because right now, building a culture of ownership is the most serious challenge facing almost every organization in America—for that matter, every organization in the world."

Corey thought for a long time before speaking again. "I've never really thought about it this way, but not only have we never designed our ideal cultural blueprint and then created the structures and processes to build that culture, we actually have more than a few structures and procedures that undermine what I think our culture should be. We talk about empowering people, and then we saddle them with rules that treat them like children. I'm beginning to think that one of my first priorities should be to work with the leadership team to define our ideal culture and evaluate our current structures and processes for how well they do or don't help us support that culture—then, of course, to design new structures and processes that will help us achieve that ideal."

Walt nodded. "I think that would be a very good thing for you to do. But first, you need to begin at the beginning."

"What do you mean? Where's the beginning?"

"Come on, let's take a trip."

5 | Lesson 3: Build Culture on a Foundation of Values

"Have you ever wondered what it would be like to be a fly on the wall?" Walt and Corey were walking on a path that snaked its way through a forest with trees so tall they stretched beyond sight, seemingly into the clouds above.

"You mean like in one of those science-fiction movies, where a man shrinks down to microscopic proportions?" Corey recalled having once seen a movie based on that premise, which he thought had been a Disney production, though at that moment he couldn't for the life of him remember the title.

"Yeah, like that. To be able to fly into a room unnoticed, perch on a wall, and eavesdrop on people. Have you ever wondered what that would be like?"

"No, Walt, I really can't say that I have—at least not seriously enough to try and concoct weird shrinking potions in our experimental kitchen."

"Hmmm." Walt shoved his hands deeper into his pockets as they walked along. "I have."

"You've wondered what it would be like to be a fly on the wall?"

"No. I've *been* a fly on the wall. It's wonderfully entertaining— and if you're in the right room, you can learn a lot as well. Would you like to try it?"

Corey shook his head and laughed. "No, I don't think so. My wife says that I should lose a little weight, but I don't think turning myself into a bug is what she has in mind. Besides, I have a mortal fear of flyswatters."

"You've got to put your hands in your pockets."

"Excuse me?"

"You've got to stick your hands in your pockets to give the wings space to grow. Like this." Walt jingled the change in his pockets.

Corey laughed again and rolled his eyes. "Whatever you say, Walt." He shoved his hands down into his pockets.

"Whatever you do, be still. Of all the offices in the world, this is the one where you least want to be caught being a fly." Corey didn't hear the words but rather felt the message. He tried to look at Walt but saw everything as though looking through a kaleidoscope. Gradually, his eyes adjusted, and he saw that he was looking down upon a very large office. At the end of the room was a big desk that was perfectly clear but for a telephone, an old-fashioned dictation machine, and one neat pile of paper. Behind the desk sat a tall, thin man in a perfectly tailored suit.

"That's General Robert Wood Johnson, chairman of Johnson & Johnson. He has a pathological aversion to bugs, so keep your wings tucked in." Corey swiveled his head to where Walt Disney should have been. Instead of seeing Walt, there was a fly—another fly—on the wall. "Now pay attention," the fly said in Walt's voice, "you're about to learn an important lesson. The year is 1963, and this is the first of four J&J meetings we will attend."

There was a soft knock at the office door. A much younger man stepped in and walked slowly toward the big desk. "You wanted to see me, sir?"

General Johnson looked up from his paperwork. "Mr. Burke, I understand that you made a bad decision about a product that has cost this company a great deal of money. Is that true?"

"Yes, sir," the younger man said, and he appeared to be bracing himself for a storm.

General Johnson stood up, came around from his desk, and extended his right hand. "Congratulations. Making decisions is what business is all about, and you don't make decisions without making mistakes. Don't ever make that mistake again, Mr. Burke, but please be sure you make other mistakes. I need people like you to make up for those who don't have the gumption to make mistakes because they're afraid to take risks at all."

A sudden fog passed through the room, obscuring everything. When it passed, General Johnson was sitting at his desk writing, only now he looked much younger than he had before. It was obviously late, because the lamp was on and it was dark outside. "We're back to 1946," Walt said. "General Johnson is working on a document that will become known as the J&J Credo. It describes in detail the company's responsibilities to five key constituencies. Those are, in this order, customers, employees, management, communities, and stockholders. To this day, the J&J Credo is generally considered to be one of the finest statements of company values and corporate responsibilities ever written."

The fog returned, and General Johnson disappeared from view. When the fog dissipated, Walt and Corey were looking down upon a large board room. There were about 25 managers in the room. At the front of the room stood James Burke, whom Corey recognized as an older version of the man Robert Wood Johnson had congratulated for making a costly mistake. "That is my challenge to all of you," Burke said to the group. "If we do not believe in the credo, if we are not all willing to abide by it—even when that means making tough decisions that might cost this company a lot of money—and if you are not telling your people to live by it, then let's take it off the walls and throw it away."

Walt said, "The year is 1976, and Burke is now president of Johnson & Johnson. His managers took him up on what came to be known as the Credo Challenge, and in the next several years, tens of thousands of J&J employees went through training on the credo. At the time, no one could have known just how important that would be."

The fog passed through the room once more, and when it cleared, the room was again filled with managers, many of whom Corey recognized from the previous meeting. James Burke was again at the front of the room, though he looked older and a lot more tired this time. "The year is 1982," Walt said. "The company has just learned that seven people were murdered in Chicago by a psychopath who somehow laced cyanide into Tylenol capsules on drugstore shelves. As you can see, it has been emotionally devastating for people in this company."

"How certain can we be that the problem is limited to Chicago?" Burke asked one of his managers.

"Quite certain," replied a man who looked like he hadn't slept in three days. "I'd say ninety-nine percent."

Burke thought about that for a moment, then said, "That's not good enough. Pull it off the shelves—everywhere, coast to coast."

"It's going to cost a lot of money," someone else said. "Probably in the tens of millions of dollars."

Burke picked up a copy of the credo, which had been placed in front of each chair, and read the first line aloud: "We believe our first responsibility is to the doctors, nurses, and patients, to mothers and fathers and all others who use our products and services." He laid down the credo and looked around the room. "If we really believe this, then ninety-nine percent just isn't good enough, is it? Pull it from the shelves; tell our customers everywhere to return capsules for a refund or replacement with tablets. We'll worry about paying for it later."

"That decision did cost J&J tens of millions of dollars," Walt said. "But in retrospect, not only was it the right thing to do, it also quite inadvertently turned out to be one of the most brilliant marketing decisions ever made. The bond of trust that J&J established with customers by the way it handled the Tylenol crisis is of incalculable value. And the pride, and sense of ownership, it created among J&J employees was priceless. They even started a 'We're Coming Back!' campaign. As with the train crash at Port Jervis that Tom Watson used to reinforce corporate culture, the Tylenol crisis, which could have been devastating to customer loyalty and employee morale, actually created incredible goodwill on both fronts."

"Yes," Corey replied, "I remember now having read the case study when I was in business school."

"To this day, the credo serves as a guide for how J&J people should conduct their daily business. And though that was not the original purpose, it is still one of the most effective marketing tools ever devised. Customers want to do business with a company they know they can trust to do the right thing. And the most talented people want to work for a company where values are a living, breathing part of the cultural fabric, not just words posted up on the wall until the next CEO comes on board and decides to rewrite them."

Corey nodded. "There's always a supply of Tylenol in our medicine cabinet, and my biz school classmates who went to work for J&J are all still there. I guess I'd never associated that sort of loyalty with the company's credo."

"So, what's the credo of Owatt Hospitality?"

Corey shrugged. "Cecil Owatt did create a statement of values that we used to have posted around here and there, but they've mostly been taken down. I doubt that anyone in the company, including me, could tell you what that statement said—much less what it means for how we should treat our customers and each other."

"So, what are you going to do about that?"

"Well, as soon as I get back from my meeting at the bank"—Corey looked at his watch; it was still 7:11—"which begins in forty-nine minutes, I'm going to look up Cecil's original statement and see how it stacks up with who we are now and with who we want to be in the future."

Walt nodded in approval, then said, "Values are like gravity. They keep you anchored. There was no gravity at Enron, no gravity at WorldCom. There's no gravity in a system that would allow someone like 'Chainsaw' Al Dunlap to rip the heart out of an organization and make millions of dollars by trashing the careers of thousands of people. Without the gravity of values, the muscle of character atrophies. It's easy, at first, moving around without the constraints of values, but as we've seen over and over in the business world, in the end, it sets the stage for disaster." Walt picked up a rock about the size of a softball and tossed it to Corey. "Think fast!"

Corey caught the rock, bobbled it several times, then finally gained a secure hold. "What's this for, Walt?"

"It's a metaphor. That rock represents the responsibilities you have just taken on, and values are the gravity that makes those responsibilities feel so heavy. It's always harder to do the right thing than it is to take the easy way."

6 | Lesson 4: Trust Is the Glue in a Culture of Ownership

Corey tossed the rock back and forth between his two hands. He considered tossing it like a shot put to see how far it would go, then thought better of it. Though he could not see them, he sensed the presence of other people nearby. He shuddered at the cosmic consequences of hitting someone in another dimension with a rock thrown from this one.

"You know what I could go for right now?" Walt asked, interrupting Corey's musings on the nature of the universe. "A cheeseburger and a chocolate shake."

"Didn't we just eat hot dogs?" Corey looked at his watch. The second hand was moving, but the watch still read 7:11 in the morning.

"Oh, that was ages ago. Besides, you should eat when you're hungry, not just when your watch tells you it's time to eat."

Corey followed Walt down the sidewalk and realized that he was indeed suddenly famished. They were headed toward a yellowish glow that grew increasingly bright. At last, Corey recognized the Golden Arches. The restaurant came into view. It was small—no inside seating, only a walk-up window. The two arches stood over the building like twin rainbows over a meadow. It looked like photos Corey had seen of the very first McDonald's back in the fifties. "Wow, McDonald's has really gone retro. This looks just like the earliest stores." Walt smiled but didn't comment.

As they walked toward the building, Corey noticed a man in a suit and tie who was on his hands and knees, scraping a piece of gum off the walkway with a car key. Looking closer, Corey could see he was quite a bit older than the typical McDonald's employee. Several days earlier, the Owatt human relations director had given a presentation to the executive team about what he'd called the coming employee drought, in which there would be far too many jobs chasing far too few good workers. He'd said that the real crisis would hit in about 10 years. One of the strategies they'd be forced to consider was raising salaries high enough to attract retired people to come back and work in frontline jobs like housekeeping. *I must be seeing that back-to-the-future moment here*, Corey thought to himself.

The man in the suit had dumped the gum into a trash can and was now picking up papers in the parking lot. Corey looked at Walt. "I guess all those forecasts about a coming labor shortage have played out when McDonald's has to hire retired businessmen as janitors. What is this, about ten years in the future?"

Walt folded his arms and watched as the man pulled a handkerchief from his suit coat pocket and began polishing a smudge off one of the glass windows. "Actually, Corey, this is 1961. And the guy who's policing the grounds is none other than Ray Kroc himself—the man who started it all. More than anyone else, Ray is the person who established fast food as an industry, franchising as an accepted business model, standardization as a philosophy for quality management, and the hamburger as an icon of American culture. He was also a good friend. We drove ambulances together during the war."

"The Vietnam War?"

Walt looked at Corey as if he had just misspelled his own name in a spelling bee. "World War I."

The man Disney had identified as Ray Kroc was headed toward the back of the building. "Let's go see what happens," Walt said, and the two men hurried along in Kroc's wake.

Just inside the back door, Kroc was speaking with a man who had on a starched white shirt, apron, and white paper cap with red trim. His nametag proclaimed him to be a manager named Roger. Ray and Roger were inspecting a hamburger bun with the same sort of care a gem merchant would use to inspect a diamond.

A third man, wearing an ill-fitting suit and mismatched tie, stood off to the side, fidgeting with his ring as he watched the other two men talk. Kroc pressed a finger down through the bun, then raised it to his nose and sniffed. He broke off a piece and put it in his mouth, then handed the bun to Roger, who repeated the process. Ray looked inquisitively at Roger, who gave a slight nod of the head.

"Okay, Chuck," Kroc said to the nervous man off to the side, "you've got the business."

"Super! We're going to do a great job for you guys." Chuck opened his portfolio and retrieved a sheaf of papers. "I went ahead and drew up a contract—you know, just to keep things simple." He handed the agreement to Kroc.

"I'll tell you what, Chuck: Let's really keep things simple." Kroc ripped the contract in two and dumped the pieces into the trash, then stuck out his right hand. "At McDonald's, we only work with people we trust. A handshake will do." Chuck beamed as the two men shook hands.

"Let's go get those cheeseburgers," Walt said, motioning for Corey to follow him. Ray, Roger, and Chuck continued their conversation, having taken no notice of the coming or going of Corey and Walt. They walked past the grill, where one cook was flipping burger patties and another was squirting on precise portions of condiments before sending them forward to be wrapped. On the other side of the grill, Corey noticed that there were four cheeseburgers sitting in the bin. Walt pulled out two and handed one to Corey, but when he looked back at the bin, the same four cheeseburgers were still there. "Curiouser and curiouser," he muttered as he unwrapped his burger. It might have been an ethereal wisp of air to the young men working the cash registers at the counter, but to Corey, it was the same delicious cheeseburger he'd grown to love as a teenager.

"That handshake back there was the biggest order Chuck's little bread company has ever received," Walt said. "He's really sticking his neck out for this one. He's going to have to build a new addition onto his plant, with no greater guarantee than a handshake from Ray Kroc that the McDonald's orders are going to come through for him if he does build. It will take him years to make that investment pay off."

"Will he do it?"

"Do what?"

"Make it pay off?"

"Today, Chuck's bakery is one of the ten largest in the country. Chuck is retired and lives beside a golf course in Tucson; his daughter Barbara is president of the company. They're still the exclusive supplier of buns for all of the McDonald's stores in this region, and they still have nothing more than a handshake agreement between them."

"That's trust," Corey said. "Radical trust."

"Have you read *The Speed of Trust* by Stephen M.R. Covey?" Corey mumbled something about it being one of the books in his "to be read" pile. "Well, that one you should move from the 'good intentions' pile to the 'getting it done' pile, because you can't build a culture of ownership without great trust all the way around. Covey says that the absence of trust is like a tax on your business. When there's no trust, everything takes longer and costs more. Just think of the time and money Ray and Chuck saved by not having to hire an army of lawyers, accountants, and consultants to help them do this deal."

"It's going to take us a long while to build that sort of trust at Owatt, Walt—if it's possible at all." Corey shook his head. The company was currently in litigation with a builder over one of its hotel properties and engaged in a nasty fight with a labor union.

"There was probably something else you didn't catch in that exchange. The agreement is between Chuck's bakery and the McDonald's Corporation, but the buns are going to be delivered to Roger, the franchisee. The company won't take a markup, and any rebates will go directly to Roger, not to the company. Ray was a very tough competitor, but he also knew that his competition should be with other burger joints, not with his franchisees or suppliers. Kroc often referred to McDonald's as a three-legged stool, with the three legs being the company, its franchisees, and its suppliers."

"A real win-win," Corey said as he watched the precision with which the fry man was slicing, washing, blanching, frying, bagging, and then salting the french fries.

"Yes, but I don't think Ray would have approved of that term, 'win-win.'"

"You're kidding. Why not?"

"Well, when it came to the franchisees and suppliers he considered to be his partners, Ray's attitude seemed to be more like 'First you win, and then I win.' He had this visceral understanding that if those partners were successful, then he'd be successful. Considering how successful he was, he must have been on to something." Walt smiled nostalgically as if remembering the days when McDonald's and Disneyland were both helping to redefine California culture. "On at least one occasion, McDonald's suppliers bailed out the company with loans when it was at risk of going under. I can't think of another example of that ever happening in the business world."

"When I had my first job at McDonald's," Corey said, "the owner talked about how the company was like a big family. In fact, he called it his McFamily."

"In recent years, it's become vogue for business executives to focus on strategy and accountability. If you're going to bring Owatt back to its former greatness, I don't think you'll do it with brilliant strategies and by holding people's feet to the fire to pursue those strategies." Walt made a face as if he were in great pain. "Ouch! Think of the metaphors we use for accountability—holding someone's feet to the fire! No wonder people are so resistant to even that word, 'accountability.' No, Corey, you need to take a page from the book of McDonald's. Think 'First you win, and then I win' rather than win-win, and think family rather than corporate."

"That sounds pretty countercultural, Walt. Hmm, now there's an interesting paradox: Build a strong culture by going counter-culture."

"There's a great saying that's been making the rounds lately: 'Culture eats strategy for lunch.' Enron had a brilliant strategy but was brought down by a horribly flawed culture. Over the years, McDonald's has tried some pretty seriously flawed strategies—does anyone remember Ray Kroc's Hula-Burger?—but a uniquely powerful culture has assured that none of them were fatal."

Corey thought for a minute, then said, "I was recently reading a book about human motivation. It said that accountability is extrinsic, because its source is having someone else look over your shoulder—or hold your feet to the fire. Pride of ownership, on the other hand, is intrinsic because the source is your own commitment. It just struck me that this is analogous to strategy, which is extrinsically motivating, and culture, which is intrinsically motivating."

"Why don't you play with that thought a bit more," Walt said. "Hey, they're starting a staff meeting in the back. Let's go listen in." Corey followed Walt back past the grill.

Ray and Roger were standing against the wall; the rest of the crew were sitting on boxes or on the floor. Roger's assistant manager was left up front to man the counter. Roger was first to speak. "You all know Mr. Kroc."

"Please, everyone, call me Ray," Kroc interjected.

"You all saw Ray out front picking up 'our' parking lot." Roger crossed his arms and looked at his young crew in the way a parent might scowl at a child who'd just come home with an F on his report card. Then his face softened, and he said, "Ray won't have to do that the next time he visits, will he?" Heads shook, and Corey could tell just from the body language where each individual fell on what he called the attitude bell curve—whether they were really buying into being a part of the McFamily or would rather be anywhere else in the world but couldn't walk out of the meeting because they needed the paycheck.

"We have four core values at McDonald's," Ray said. "Who can tell me what they are?"

Without thinking, Corey raised his hand, then sheepishly brought it back down when he realized that no one in the room could see him. Walt looked at him with raised eyebrows. "You still remember them? How long has it been?"

"Thirty-two years. And yes, the manager pounded 'QVSC' so deeply into my brain that I'll never forget it: quality, value, service, and cleanliness."

Most of the workers raised their hands. Ray pointed to someone who didn't. "Jerry," he said, reading the nametag on the young man's apron, "how long have you been working with us?"

The young man shrugged. "I dunno, 'bout a month. Maybe two."

Kroc narrowed his focus as if trying to see through the young man's skin to what was on the inside. "Let me tell you something, Jerry. We didn't hire you to be a burger flipper." Jerry's face registered surprise. "No, we hired you to serve our customers a good meal at a great price in a clean restaurant. Quality, value, service, and cleanliness are our values here at McDonald's, Jerry, but they're also your job." Now Kroc scanned the room. "The next time I come back, I'll expect you all to know these values. And I'll expect to see them being practiced—beginning with your parking lot being a whole lot cleaner than it was when I got here today."

"Let's step outside for a minute," Walt said, giving Corey's shoulder a nudge. Once they were outside, he said, "That young man in there—Jerry—is a high school dropout who's had several run-ins with the law." Corey shook his head and looked down at his shoes. He knew the type well. There were a lot of troubled kids working for Owatt who had so much potential but who had run their lives into dead ends by the poor choices they had made. "Let's go back in now," Walt said.

Corey gasped in amazement. The room was more than twice as large as the one he and Walt had just left. The faces were all different, and instead of the white shirts and paper caps of the sixties, people were wearing the blue shirts and baseball caps he'd see when he took his kids to their local McDonald's. Ray and Roger were gone, but the man speaking at the front of the room looked vaguely familiar.

"That's Jerry," Walt said, "the kid who didn't know the values of McDonald's when Ray asked him. I guess he took Ray's comments to heart, because today, he's the manager—one of about a hundred thousand McDonald's employees who started out flipping burgers and worked their way up to management positions."

"That's a great story, Walt."

"It *is* a great story. In fact, we should talk more about telling stories to create culture. Come on, Corey, let's go for a ride—a wild ride!"

7 | Lesson 5: Use Stories to Reinforce Cultural Norms

"Hang on!" Walt and Corey were sitting side by side in the latest ride, strapped securely into their seats. With explosive acceleration, they were launched into a kaleidoscope of shapes and colors—and sounds.

"Music?" Corey looked inquisitively at Walt, then instinctively grabbed his shoulder harness as the capsule they were riding in corkscrewed through a burst of the aurora borealis.

"Yes, music!" Walt shouted. "Isn't this great?" The spacecraft hurtled onward, and Corey waited for his stomach to settle back into the accustomed space in his anatomy before nodding in agreement. "Yeah, Walt, great."

"That's Toccata and Fugue by Johann Sebastian Bach, as orchestrated by Leopold Stokowski. You've seen *Fantasia,* haven't you?"

"I think so, when I was a kid."

"Well, right now you are 'in' *Fantasia*. Oops, hang on; here we go again." The ship lurched forward and to the side, and Corey felt as much as he heard the music change, now becoming dark and wild. The craft stretched over a landscape scarred by volcanic lava flows. Corey recognized the powerful pulsations of Stravinsky's *The Rite of Spring.*

"*Fantasia* was the first movie ever to use stereophonic sound," Walt said with obvious pride. The ride smoothed out. As they flew through the chords of Beethoven's Pastoral Symphony, Corey was astonished at how profoundly a change in the music could shift his entire emotional and sensory presence. "We needed a lot of special equipment to get the sound right," Walt continued, "and we were on a tight budget. So, when we came across these two young fellows in Palo Alto who could give us the audio oscillators we needed for a much lower price, the decision was—I believe the term your generation would use is that it was a 'no-brainer.'"

"What two fellows?"

"Uh-oh, here comes trouble."

"What trouble?" The music had changed, again taking an ominous turn, and outside the capsule it was as dark as if they were buried in a mine shaft. Corey recognized the music—*Night on Bald Mountain.* "What trouble, Walt!"

"Chernabog," Walt replied, genuine concern rippling his voice. The craft banked sharply to the right. Out the left window, Corey saw a creature more hideous than his worst nightmares had ever summoned. Wings spread, it was reaching out for them. Crashing cymbals and drums punctuated the aural maelstrom. Walt was pressing hard against the controls, totally focused on a tiny speck of light at the far horizon, like a racecar driver trying to avoid a collision with the wall by keeping his eyes focused on where he wanted the car to go rather than where it was headed. The speck of light grew larger, and Corey realized it was the rising sun. Receding into the distance behind them, he could hear Chernabog bellowing in agony.

"That was a close call," Walt said.

"Good thing it was just a cartoon," Corey replied with a weak laugh.

Walt gave Corey a knowing smile. "You will find, if you pay attention, that reality can be a fairly malleable notion and that sometimes, fictional characters can be more real than real people." Walt flipped a switch on the control panel. "We'll be coming in soon."

"Coming in where?"

"Bill Hewlett and Dave Packard."

"What?"

"The two fellows I mentioned—the ones we bought the audio oscillators from. They went on to build a very successful company. You've heard of Hewlett-Packard?"

"Of course. We have HP computers and printers on just about every desk at Owatt."

"When it comes to building a culture of ownership, Bill Hewlett and Dave Packard wrote the book—almost literally. Bill-and-Dave stories are famous for having defined 'The HP Way.' You've no doubt read about it in books like *In Search of Excellence* and *Built to Last*, yes?"

Corey nodded but simultaneously made a mental note that among all the other things he'd have to do in taking on his new duties, he needed to revisit the bookshelf.

"Regardless of whether they're factually accurate, the best stories all carry a bigger truth. And the best leaders know that an important part of their job is—through their actions—to write the stories that help to define the culture of their organizations." Walt punched several buttons on the control panel, and the capsule ride opened up like a clamshell. "Well, here we are," he said as he unlatched his shoulder harness and stepped out. Corey followed suit and found himself standing on a pebblestone driveway facing a tiny garage with twin doors held shut by a single padlock.

"Where is 'here'?"

"Here is 367 Addison Street, Palo Alto, California. More precisely, here is the famous HP garage—the birthplace of Silicon Valley."

"This little shed? It's tiny."

"The seeds of great dreams often are planted in humble soil. Let's take a look inside." The double doors swung open, and the driveway became a moving walkway, carrying Walt and Corey though the garage. A desk, a drill press, a few instruments, and that was it. Within seconds, the moving walkway had passed through the garage and was now in a more contemporary business building. "You're about to see the origin of one of the most famous of all Bill-and-Dave stories," Walt said as the walkway came to a stop inside what looked like an industrial laboratory.

The room was unoccupied except for a man in a short-sleeved shirt who had just come in from a door to the right. Oblivious to the presence of Walt and Corey, he marched purposefully across the room toward a large cabinet. Putting a hand on the door of the cabinet, he realized it was locked. He glared at the padlock as though not believing what his eyes were telling his brain they were seeing. He gave the lock a tug, but it was securely clamped. After vainly scouring the surrounding countertops for a key, the man stormed out of the room.

"Who was that? And what are these?" Corey pointed to a row of glass tubes arranged across one of the counters.

"That's Bill Hewlett. And these are vacuum tubes—like the ones you would have found in your father's stereo when he was a teenager. Now, watch this."

The man in short sleeves had reentered the room, carrying a massive bolt cutter. After straining at it for the better part of a minute, he finally snipped the lock off and opened the cabinet. Hewlett pulled out something that looked like what Corey thought might have resembled his father's childhood radio; then, he hung the now-useless lock back on the clasp. He went to one of the countertops and in big, angry letters scribbled on a piece of graph paper:

We trust each other at Hewlett-Packard.
Never lock this door again!

As the walkway started moving again, Corey saw Hewlett taping his sign on the cabinet door. "Do you think that door ever got locked again?" Walt asked.

"Not as long as Bill and Dave were around!" Corey replied.

"It takes great courage to build an organization on a foundation of radical trust like that. There's always the risk that you'll be taken advantage of. Stories help to reinforce the norms. But what happens when people forget to tell stories like this?"

"Hmm, I do recall that there was some sort of scandal after Fiorina left HP. Wasn't the head of the board indicted for spying on other board members or something like that?

"Something like that," Walt replied. "When they stopped telling the stories, they forgot the lessons. And then they got into trouble."

The moving walkway was pausing over a large office area. Looking down, Corey saw a beehive of activity: people working on projects in their cubicles, talking on the telephone, gathered in small groups at chalkboards and flip charts. "It's a Friday afternoon in 1970. Do you see anything that strikes you as unusual in this Hewlett-Packard operation?"

Corey pursed his lips and looked harder. "No, Walt, everyone seems to be working pretty hard."

"Yep, and that's what's unusual. If you know your business history, 1970 was a very tough year for Silicon Valley. Most companies responded to the crisis with mass layoffs. At HP, Bill Hewlett decided to share the sacrifice—just as he and Dave had previously agreed to share their success—by asking people to take off every other Friday without pay. It became known as the nine-day fortnight. This is one of those Fridays. *Now* does anything strike you as unusual?"

"Well, if all those guys are still working even though they're not getting paid, I'd say that's pretty unusual—very unusual!"

"It's a paradox we'll see in every company that has successfully built a culture of ownership. When you trust people to act in the best interest of the company and when you place long-term loyalty ahead of short-term profits, you can create a sustainable and unrivalled source of competitive advantage. Think about it, Corey. What do you think is going on this Friday afternoon at all of those competing companies that have gone through mass layoffs? Better yet, I'll show you."

The moving walkway was now passing over another office complex filled with cubicles. About a quarter of the cubicles were empty, but people who were in their cubicles seemed to be working very intently. "This is one of HP's competitors," Walt said. "Do you see anything unusual here?"

"They all seem to be working hard. I guess it doesn't really matter whether they're working hard because they care about the company or they're just afraid of losing their jobs, as long as the work's getting done."

Walt looked at Corey the way one might look at a grown man who'd just asked where babies come from. "Take a closer look," Walt instructed, handing Corey a pair of binoculars.

Corey focused in on a man who was intensely concentrating on the document he was drafting; then he narrowed in on the document itself. "It's his resume!" Corey exclaimed. He moved the binoculars to another cubicle and saw another resume being revised. He was about to look at a third cubicle when a man at the far end of the room stuck his head above the partition of his cubicle and hollered, "Has anyone got a slide rule?" Instantly, resumes were slammed away into desk drawers or shoved under piles of paper to be replaced by graph paper, three-ring binders, and computer printouts. A man in a suit and tie walked into the room. "Who needs a slide rule?" The newcomer pulled a slide rule from his coat pocket and gave it to the man who'd asked, then began patrolling the rest of the room.

"That's the boss," Walt said. "He knows something's going on but isn't sure what it is. He's got to cut another thirty jobs next week and just made a mental note that the lookout—the guy who asked for a slide rule—can't be trusted and needs to get a pink slip." Walt retrieved the binoculars from Corey. "Think of the irony. The people that Hewlett-Packard did *not* lay off are *not* getting paid for being in their offices today, creating the products with which they *are* going to clobber Brand X in the marketplace. Meanwhile, the people down there that Brand X *is* paying are *not* working on products to help their company compete with HP. Instead, they're working on their resumes in hopes of getting a job working for HP. Actually, when you get right down to it, by not doing the work that Brand X is paying them to do, they *already are* working for HP."

The moving walkway was now outdoors, passing over what appeared to be a beautiful park. They were looking down on a picnic; men in white aprons and chef hats were grilling steaks and burgers for a throng of hungry customers. "That's Bill and Dave and other senior HP managers, flipping burgers at a company picnic." Walt pulled an index card from his pocket and made a note, and Corey wondered if he'd just come up with an idea for a new picnic ride in his celestial theme park. Before he had a chance to ask, though, Walt said, "Bill and Dave always talked about HP being a family; so do a lot of other business leaders—including, I believe, your predecessor in the CEO is chair at Owatt Hospitality. It's nice to talk about family in the good times—much more difficult in tough times. But Bill and Dave really meant it. A real family doesn't give the youngest child a pink slip when things get tight."

The magic walkway was moving again. Looking back, Corey estimated there were at least a thousand people of all ages at the HP picnic, nestled into a clearing in the redwood forest. "The place was called Little Basin," Walt said. "Bill and Dave bought the land for just this purpose. Some of those children you see playing ball down there—they are loyal HP employees today, and through whatever hard times the company might face, they have always treasured the memory of these company outings with Bill and Dave."

The land below them mellowed, and Corey recognized the rolling vineyards of the California Wine Country. The walkway descended toward a sprawling hotel; the sign out front read Sonoma

Mission Inn. "The year is 1957," Walt said. "We're about to peek in on the first HP leadership retreat called by Bill and Dave. It was an event that both crystallized who they were as a company and set directions for their future growth. Earlier in the meeting, Dave described a process that in the years since has become known as management by objectives, or MBO." Corey nodded. They practiced a form of MBO at Owatt, though he suspected it was a very different process than that introduced by Bill and Dave; at Owatt, the CEO set the objectives, and everyone else went to work trying to meet them. "Now," Walt continued, "he's describing the corporate objectives that would guide Hewlett-Packard for many years to come."

There were about 25 men in the hotel conference room. Corey recognized Bill and Dave from photos he'd seen of the pair. Dave, who was every bit the commanding physical presence he'd been reported to be, was speaking from the front of the room. "He's already covered their first four objectives," Walt said, "which are pretty much the things you'd expect of a big corporation: making a profit, serving customers, staying focused, and growing. It's the next two—or rather, the way he states the next two—that really were revolutionary and were at the heart of HP's culture of ownership." Dave folded over a page of the flip chart and in big block letters wrote:

EMPLOYEES

"Our employees make our company's success possible," he said, "and we must make the commitment to share that success with them." He made a note on the flip chart and then continued: "Since our people are our greatest asset, and it is a company's duty to preserve its assets, we need to provide our people with job security. Most importantly, we need to give them the opportunity for the personal satisfaction that comes from a sense of accomplishment in their work." Dave made a few more notes on the flip chart, then folded over to a new page. At the top, he wrote:

ORGANIZATION

"Yesterday, we decided that in order to keep alive the sense of us being like a family here at HP, we needed to establish a diversified structure so that people could work in groups small enough where they could really get to know each other. This is more than just how the organization chart is structured; it gets to the very heart of how we do business. We need to establish very broad goals for growing our business and then give our people wide latitude of freedom in working toward the accomplishment of those goals." Dave made notes on the flip chart, and most of the other men were making notes at their tables. Corey did not see any disagreement in any of the men's facial expressions or body language. They really were a team, he thought to himself.

The Sonoma Mission Inn faded away into the distance. Corey was about to ask a question, then stopped when he saw Walt was deep in thought, a somber and pensive expression on his face. At last, Walt said, "I'm sure you know that Hewlett-Packard has been through some difficult times in recent years."

"Walt, you really are a master of the subtle understatement."

Walt laughed, but his reflective expression quickly returned. "Most of the companies we're looking at—companies that one way or another were built upon commitment to a culture of ownership—hit a tough time at some point after the departure of the founder, or founders." Walt closed his eyes and sighed deeply. "Including mine."

Corey watched the California countryside pass beneath them, respecting Walt's silence. At last, the older man said, "More than anything, what caused the trouble was that each company became unmoored from its culture. Those that pulled through and regained their former greatness—the way that HP has—did so by reconnecting with that traditional culture."

"Maybe that's one of the benefits of a crisis," Corey said.

"How so?" Walt replied.

"When the ship is about to go down and the captain gives the 'all hands on deck' order, people aren't responding just because they've been commanded; they're up on deck because it's in their best interest to be there."

"It's a perfect metaphor," Walt said. "When the big storm hits, there are no job descriptions; there's only the work that needs to be done. And it becomes everyone's job to see that the work gets done—and done right. Now, if you're out on a boat in the ocean and a big storm hits, you would want to know that the sailors upon whom your life might depend knew what they were doing, wouldn't you?" Corey nodded his assent. "But you would also want to know that they had personal strength of character and that they believed in themselves, correct?"

"Absolutely!"

"It's the same thing in business—which is why it's so astonishing that so few companies invest in helping people develop those personal qualities, since the future of their businesses—not to mention their executive careers—might depend upon it. Shall we go meet a leader who understood that as well as anyone?"

"You bet!" Corey did not need any more encouragement than that.

8 | Lesson 6: Invest in Character Building

Walt and Corey were standing on a balcony, looking down upon a huge crowd of cheering women—and almost everyone in the audience was a woman. The stage was backed by three gigantic projection screens. Rock music was blaring, the dance troupe was whirling, colored lights were flashing, and a dry-ice fog drifted across the floor. An elegantly dressed young woman strolled through the mist, took the microphone in her right hand, and began singing in a voice that was three sizes too large for her body:

I have a premonition
That soars on silver wings.
It's the dream of your accomplishment
Of many wondrous things.

"Are we in Las Vegas?" Sin City had been much on Corey's mind lately. Until last year, the Desert Plum Casino had been a crown jewel in the Owatt tiara, but with the recent economic slump, sales had gone south, dragging profits with them.

"No," Walt replied, "we're in Dallas."

"Dallas? I didn't realize that Dallas had gotten into the showbiz business."

"It hasn't. This is the annual Mary Kay seminar. Every summer, more than fifty thousand Mary Kay independent beauty consultants descend upon the city; they take over the convention center for a month. Just look at that enthusiasm: If that's not a culture of ownership, I don't know what is." Walt smiled and swayed to the beat of the song:

I do not know beneath which sky
Or where you'll challenge fate.

I only know it will be high!
I only know it will be great!

The singer took a bow and blew kisses as the audience went wild. It took nearly five minutes for the emcee to regain control of the event, though Corey got the impression that he really wasn't trying very hard to quiet things down. *This guy is a real pro,* Corey thought to himself; the emcee had a fifty-dollar smile and a Hollywood voice. "And now, please help me welcome Mary Kay's newest independent national executive sales director, Lori Banacek!" She wore a floor-length sequined gown, was escorted by a young man in a tuxedo, and seemed right at home standing at a microphone in front of ten thousand screaming women.

"Thank you. Thank you all." Only now did Corey detect the slightest waver in her voice. He noticed that she was wearing a diamond-studded bumblebee brooch. "Thank you very much," she repeated, motioning for the audience to take their seats. When things had finally settled down, she said, "It's true, I am the newest national executive sales director, but this is not the first time I've stood up here in front of you all to acknowledge the fact. No. In fact, I've been here thousands of times. I've been on this stage every single day for the past twenty-four years. And today, I want to invite you all to join me up here—every single one of you—because it can be you, too." The audience again went wild, cheering, clapping, and whistling.

Banacek nodded, eyes making contact with people throughout the hall, her smile conveying a determined toughness. "I have two 'me' statements that I make every day—statements that are responsible for me being here today. Can I share those with you?" From the audience reaction, Corey thought she might as well have been offering them the keys to Fort Knox. "The first is 'Watch me.' Every time someone tells me I can't do something, I say, 'Watch me.' They'd say, 'You can't go from being just a secretary to making a six-figure income with Mary Kay,' and I'd say, 'Watch me.' They'd say, 'You can't touch the lives of thousands of women by showing them how to achieve their God-given potential in life,' and I'd say, 'Watch me.' They'd say, 'You can't be a successful businesswoman if you put God and your family ahead of your career,' and I'd say, 'You just watch me!' And I did every one of those things." With every "Watch me," the audience grew more animated. "So, now I want all of you beautiful women, and you few courageous men out there, to turn to your neighbor, and I want you to repeat after me: 'Yes, I can—watch me!'"

Ten thousand voices rose to the challenge, but it was not good enough for Lori Banacek. "I can't hear you!" The resulting roar, Corey thought, could probably have been heard in Denver. Banacek had the audience screaming "Watch me" after each affirmation she shouted from the stage. "Yes, I can change my life—watch me! Yes, I can put God first, family second, and career third—watch me! Yes, I can drive a pink Cadillac—watch me!"

When things finally settled down and everyone had retaken their seats, Banacek stepped back up to the microphone. "The second 'me' statement is 'Let me.' Let me help you feel good about yourself; let me show you how to build your business; let me be a part of your life and your family. If you want to be up here on this stage one day, and I sincerely hope you all do, then your every 'Watch me' has to be followed by a 'Let me,' because the only way you will ever make your dreams come true is by helping others make their dreams come true."

Banacek signaled to the emcee, who was waiting at the left of the stage, and then spoke into the microphone. "Now, would you all join me in a song? You know the words, don't you?" The music started, and Banacek, in a voice that Corey thought was better than many of the lounge singers he'd hired over the years, led the group:

I've got that Mary Kay enthusiasm down in my heart.

Looking out over the crowd, Corey saw that every single person knew the words of the song and were putting their hearts into its singing. He also knew enough about Mary Kay to know that not only were they not being paid to be there, but they had paid their own way to attend. He tried to imagine ten thousand Owatt employees singing together, having paid their own way to fly to Dallas, but the picture would not materialize.

Walt tugged on Corey's sleeve. "Would you like to see the first time Lori Banacek saw herself on this stage twenty-four years ago?"

Corey shrugged. "Sure, why not?"

And just like that, the world started to rewind—slowly at first, as the Mary Kay enthusiasm song played itself in reverse and Lori Banacek walked backward off the stage, and then in a blinding blur of sight and sound. When things finally slowed and stopped, Walt and Corey were looking into an executive office. Two women were sitting on a sofa. Corey recognized Mary Kay Ash from the cover of a book she'd written. The other woman looked like a much younger Lori Banacek. She was in tears.

"I can't, Mary Kay. It's just not working. I don't think I'm cut out for this."

"Really?" Mary Kay registered genuine surprise. "Do you think God has a special pair of scissors that cut you out to be something else?"

Lori laughed through her tears, and Mary Kay handed her a Kleenex. "No, of course not. I don't know; my husband really doesn't support me. He thinks it's ridiculous."

"What does your husband do?"

"He's a medical student. He's in his fourth year. Next year, he starts a surgery residency."

"Is that so? He's going to be a doctor, and he thinks what we're doing is ridiculous? That's odd, don't you think? We're trying to do the same thing he is—make people feel better. It's just that we're trying to make them feel better about themselves. If a woman doesn't feel good about herself—well, that requires doctoring of a different sort, doesn't it?"

Banacek sniffled and nodded. "I like that part, Mary Kay—the part about helping other women. But I don't like selling. I just can't seem to get that right."

"And why have you chosen to not like selling? Nothing happens until someone sells something, you know. You have to sell your children on making their beds in the morning; your husband has to sell his patients on throwing away their cigarettes. We all have to sell, Lori. There are two kinds of people in the world: people who are in sales and know they're in sales, who take it seriously and learn to be effective and get what they want out of life, and people who are in sales but think they're not, who would never dream of reading a book or taking a class, and then wonder why things aren't working out for them. So, you just have to choose which one of those two sorts of people you want to be."

"I know," Banacek sniffed, "but . . ."

Mary Kay touched Banacek's knee. "There's no 'but,' Lori. When you get home today, I want you to take out your Bible and I want you to read the story in Mark 9:23. Jesus said that all things are possible for one who believes. If you read the story, though, you'll see that you don't have to have total belief; you just have to have enough to overcome your unbelief. You've got to have enthusiasm if you want to accomplish great things, but the fuel for that enthusiasm is belief—believing in yourself and in your mission in life. You've got to break through your belief barriers."

"I know," Banacek replied, not sounding at all convinced.

Mary Kay got up and walked over to her desk. She returned carrying a small white box and a pad of paper. Handing the pad to Banacek, she said, "I want you to write down the names and telephone numbers of ten friends and neighbors, Lori. And while you do that, let me show you what I have for you." It took her a moment to get started, and she had to check several names in her date-book, but Banacek finally wrote down 10 names and corresponding telephone numbers.

Mary Kay opened the small white box and pulled out a diamond-studded pin in the shape of a bumblebee. "You know, Lori, aerospace engineers tell us that a bumblebee should not be able to fly. The wings aren't big and strong enough for the body. But don't you ever tell a bumblebee that she can't fly, and don't you ever let anyone—including yourself—tell you that you can't fly." Mary Kay put the pin back in the box and set it aside. "I'm going to give you that pin, Lori, but not today; I'm going to give it to you at the seminar in front of thousands of other women. And I'm going to give it to you because you've earned it. Now, let me see your list."

Banacek handed over the pad with her list of names. Mary Kay scanned the page, then said, "I've got a group of business school students coming here in about fifteen minutes, but we should have time to make these calls." She motioned toward the telephone. "Let me help you figure out why what you're doing isn't working as well as you'd like. Go ahead and call the first person on your list. I'll listen in. Then we'll make whatever changes we need to make to get it right before you place the next call. You'll be flying in no time."

A visible change came over Banacek as she picked up the phone. Her back straightened, and her jaw jutted. "Watch me," she said under her breath, and somehow Corey knew that the words had been meant for her husband. Mary Kay listened in as Banacek made her first call—and her first appointment.

"Would you like to stick around and hear what Mary Kay has to say to the students?" Walt asked the question without taking his eyes off Lori Banacek as she made her next sales call under the watchful eye of Mary Kay.

Corey looked at his watch. It was still 7:11. "Sure, Walt, it looks like we'll have time to do that." Lori Banacek was beaming as she left Mary Kay's office. She stopped once to look back at the little white box with the diamond pin in the shape of a bumblebee and whispered "Watch me" before she exited.

Now, six students from the Baylor business school were seated in Mary Kay's office: four young men and two young women. One of the men started the conversation. "Our professor laughed when he told us to look for a parking lot full of pink Cadillacs, but there really are a lot of pink cars out there."

"He's sort of a left-brain guy," one of the women said. "I think he thinks the pink Cadillac is a silly gimmick."

"Does he, now?" Mary Kay said. "When you get back to campus, why don't you ask him what color Cadillac Baylor is giving him this year?" Everyone laughed, and Mary Kay continued. "It's an important point. People in business too often forget that one of the leader's most important roles is that of cheerleader. Some of the managers I meet from other companies are so dead serious, they seem to be seriously dead—they just haven't stopped breathing so that we can bury them without breaking the law." This earned an even bigger round of laughter. "People must be motivated. Leaders provide external motivation with praise and recognition—including, in our company, pink Cadillacs—and that, in turn, helps to fuel the internal motivation of pride in oneself and in the work one does."

"Can you tell us more about your management philosophy?" This question was from another of the young men.

"Certainly. We believe that you build a great business by focusing on P&L—people and love. Our entire business is based on the Golden Rule—that you do unto others as you would have them do unto you. I'm sure you've read about our company in preparation for this meeting, and you know that our mission is to enrich the lives of women and to give them the opportunity to build a successful career where they can put God first, family second, and career last. Now, I know that some people in the business school world think that's squishy, but I can tell you that our independent beauty consultants who set their priorities in that order are not only the happiest, but they also make the most money."

Another of the young men laughed and shook his head. "I'm a working student, and I wish you could talk to my boss. His idea of people and love is that he loves to yell at people. I mean, most of us are scared to death of him."

"He wouldn't make it at Mary Kay. We don't believe in, and won't tolerate, management by intimidation—not only because it's wrong, but also because it's very shortsighted. If people fear the boss more than they fear the competition, then eventually, the competition will win. If they fear losing a job more than they fear losing a customer, they will eventually behave in ways that cause the company to lose customers. That, of course, might end up causing them to lose their jobs, anyway."

"What are the qualities you think are most important for a leader?" It was the other young woman who asked this question.

"Very high on the list is charisma, but I should say what I mean by that term, since it's different than what you might think. I always tell my independent beauty consultants to imagine that every person they meet has a sign that says 'Make Me Feel Important.' That's what the best leaders do: They make people feel important. That's charisma. It has nothing to do with you and everything to do with how you make other people feel."

"What are the most important elements of a successful business?" This was asked by the young man who'd started the conversation with his comment about pink Cadillacs.

Mary Kay steepled her fingers under her chin for a moment. "If I had to choose one, it would be loyalty. At Mary Kay, we like to say that you know a company by the people it keeps. Loyalty is to our company what gravity is to the solar system—it keeps everything from flying apart. We express our loyalty to our independent sales force by working hard for their success, and we earn their loyalty—and frankly, expect it—by caring for them as people, not just moneymakers."

The young man who had yet to speak raised a finger, and Mary Kay nodded at him. "In our case study, I read that you were quoted as saying that 'a mediocre idea that inspires people will be more successful than a great idea that doesn't inspire people.' But do you really think a mediocre idea can ultimately be successful, even if it gets people fired up?"

"Well, Jonathan, that's a valid observation." Before she'd even finished her sentence, it was obvious that the young man was impressed, and flattered, that Mary Kay had remembered his name. "If people are inspired by a mediocre idea, they'll be motivated to try to make something happen with that idea, won't they?" Jonathan nodded in agreement. "But because it's a mediocre idea, it won't quite work out, will it?" He nodded again, now clearly unsure of where she was going with this. "But because they are inspired by the idea, they'll keep working on it, modifying it where necessary, until it does work, won't they?" He nodded again, less hesitantly this time. "It's what we call 'failing your way forward to success.' During my career, I've seen very few brilliant ideas that came out of the shell that way, but I've seen a lot of mediocre ideas that became brilliant because someone was inspired enough to keep working at the idea until it worked."

Mary Kay looked over at the clock. "We're going to have to wrap up in a minute, so let me close with this final comment about leadership: We need leaders who add value to the people and the organizations they lead; who work for the benefit of others and not just for their own personal gain; who inspire and motivate rather than intimidate and manipulate; who live with people to know their problems and live with God in order to solve them; and who follow a moral compass that points in the right direction, regardless of the trends." She smiled sweetly and said, "Go back and tell your professor *that's* what he should be teaching his students."

As the students stood to leave, the scene started to speed up. "Let's get back to the convention center so we can hear Lori's closing comments," Walt said. He held on to Corey's elbow as they flew forward through time.

Back on their balcony at the Dallas Convention Center, Corey could see that the crowd had lost none of its enthusiasm, though Walt had told him what a grueling week they'd just been through. Lori Banacek was back at the microphone. "I'd like to leave you with two thoughts. The first is from our dear departed friend, Mary Kay. When I left her office twenty-four years ago, Mary Kay told me to expect a miracle. She also told me that miracles are meant to be shared—that they don't keep well when you keep them to yourself. Some of you ladies have one of the pins that Mary Kay had made with two shovels, one bigger than the other. The small shovel represents that which you shovel out to others, and the big one represents what God shovels back into your life. There's a saying that I share with my girls: 'Help one, help two.' It's a variation on the Golden Rule: Any time you help someone else, you are helping yourself, and any time you ask someone else for their help, you are also helping them, because people love to be needed."

Banacek smiled and blew a kiss at a man in the front row. "The second thought is from my husband, Fred, who is a surgeon. When he was in his residency, he learned a saying: 'See one, do one, teach one.' That's also great advice for your Mary Kay business. Ask your sisters in this hall what is working for them—see one. Then, go out and do it yourself—do one. Then, share your story with the rest of us—teach one. Leadership at its best is teachership, and we are all called to be leaders. Thank you, and God bless you all."

Walt and Corey were now watching from their balcony as an army of men in blue jumpsuits stacked chairs and swept up paper. "You know, Walt, one of our vice presidents at Owatt thinks that Mary Kay is a cult. But if that's the sort of enthusiasm you see in a cult, I want to buy it by the truckload."

"You don't have to buy it, Corey. In fact, you *can't* buy it. You have to earn that sort of enthusiasm. But if you can, it's the ultimate 'everybody wins' outcome. Of course, Owatt wins because you'll do a better job of selling and serving customers. Your customers win because they get a better guest experience. Your employees win because they get a more positive work experience. And even your employees' families win because we tend to bring our attitudes from work home with us. Given all that, why *wouldn't* you want Owatt to be more like Mary Kay?"

"I can't think of any reason, Walt."

Walt nodded in agreement. "Neither can I." He shook his head sadly. "Have you seen the cartoon strip Dilbert?"

Corey laughed. "Of course I have—everyone's seen Dilbert. Half the cubicles in our corporate offices are festooned with Dilbert cartoons."

"It's pathetic, really," Walt said, shaking his head more emphatically. "Cartoons should lift people up, not drag them down. And Dilbert himself—that man is seriously neurotic. I call his condition Dilbert Disease."

"Dilbert Disease?"

"Yep. It's the condition of simultaneously hating your job, despising your boss, and having contempt for your coworkers—the way Dilbert does—and then being scared to death of losing that hateful job and being liberated from having to associate with all those people you can't stand." Walt shuddered involuntarily.

"Dilbert is a very sick man. And millions of workers actually think he's a hero. It's no wonder there's so much unhappiness in the workplace."

"I guess I'd never really thought of Dilbert that way—in fact, sometimes I myself find it funny. Maybe because Scott Adams can hit pretty close to home."

Walt shoved his hands into his pockets and looked off into the distance. "That's why cynics are so dangerous. They see real problems and, because they are so talented at caricature, blow them way out of proportion. I mean seriously, has there ever been a boss, no matter how nasty, who ordered a subordinate to eat a bug the way the pointed-haired boss did in one Dilbert strip? So they exaggerate the problem and make us laugh at people—not with people but *at* them. Then they jump ship. They're too lazy, or too cowardly, to be part of the solution. Their only joy is in complaining about the problems."

"The cynics sure do kill creativity," Corey said.

"Of course they do. The origin of the word is from the Greek Kynicos—which literally means 'like a dog'. Cynics are like wild dogs who never build a thing but excel at tearing things apart."

"I've always thought that it takes the positive affect of about six enthusiastic and creative people to offset the deadening impact of one cynic," Cory said.

Walt nodded in agreement. You can dream, create, design, and build the most wonderful place in the world, but you've got to have great people to make the dream into a reality. If you make the investment in helping people to develop personal skills and strength of character, the real payoff will be that they'll bring their best ideas and creativity to the job. It takes a lot of courage to be creative, which is why so few people are. I'll tell you what: Let's go visit a place that taps into people's creativity better than any organization I know."

9 | Lesson 7: Unleash Individual Creativity and Ingenuity

As the two men walked along what appeared to be a country road, Walt stooped and picked up a yellow piece of paper that had a handwritten note on it. "Hmm, listen to this, Corey: *'The difference between courageous and cowardly is usually evident only long after the fact.'* We'll, isn't that the truth. Most people thought I'd gone out of my mind when I decided to build Disneyland. Then they all said I was a genius after it was successful." He stuffed the note into Corey's shirt pocket.

After a few more steps, Corey saw another yellow piece of paper on the ground. Picking it up, he realized it was a Post-it note, also with someone's handwritten message. "Hey, Walt, this one could have been written about building a culture of ownership. Listen! *'Fear excludes and creates enemies; courage includes and creates friends.'* Whenever I see cliques and silos in an organization, I know that it's a fear-filled workplace. It takes courage to tear down those walls. I wonder who wrote these."

"Here's another one," Walt said as he bent over to scoop up several more yellow notes. " *'Fear is a reaction; courage is a decision.'* How true. Everyone faces fear. The difference is what action you decide to take in the face of that fear. And listen to this one—I hadn't really thought of the connection between caring and courage, but they are two of the most important qualities for a successful business: *'Caring is the root of courage, because when you care enough about something, you'll find the courage to do what needs to be done.'* Isn't that wonderful?"

Corey picked up another note and read aloud: *"Fear is many tomorrows; courage is one today."* Shrugging his shoulders, he asked, "What do you suppose that one means, Walt?"

"Hmm. It sounds like a variation on the 'Be Today, See Tomorrow' theme—keep your attention in the present, and keep your vision in the future. So, I think what it means is that it takes courage to not dwell on all the bad things that might happen in the future but instead to focus your energy on doing those things that need to be done right now to help you bring about your desired future."

Corey picked up several more sticky notes and read the one on top: *"Action is the hacksaw that cuts through the prison bars of fear."* Looking up, he saw that the road was covered with yellow paper as far as he could see into the distance. "Who do you suppose went to the trouble of laying down all this paper?"

Walt laughed as he handed his small collection of notes to Corey. "I think these were meant for you, Corey, and that whoever wrote them wants us to follow the yellow-note road." He bent over and picked up a few more. "Here's a good one: *'Make fear your ally by letting it catalyze you to take action instead of allowing it to paralyze you into inaction.'* A lot of the short-term thinking you see in business today is caused by executives who are paralyzed by their anxiety over quarterly results. You'll never see a culture of ownership in an organization where the boss can't see more than three months into the future."

Corey read the next note in his pile. "This one has an author's name to it. Have you ever heard of McZen?"

"Nope, can't say that I have. What does it say?"

Corey read, *"Someone with a job is never secure; someone with a calling is never unemployed."*

"That was certainly my experience," Walt replied with another laugh. "I sometimes didn't have a job, but I never lacked for work. If you have an organization filled with people who are worried about hanging on to their jobs, they'll never really take ownership for the work itself. But in any organization where people feel like it's their calling to be there doing their work, you'll be such a strong competitor that job security will take care of itself. It's a real paradox. I like this guy, McZen—do you have any more by him?"

Corey shuffled through the yellow notes he'd picked up. "Here's one: *'The journey of a thousand miles begins with a long inward gaze.'* What do you suppose that means?"

"It's pretty obvious, don't you think? You are about to embark upon a journey of a thousand miles, building a culture of ownership at Owatt Hospitality. But before you take the first step forward, you have to take a long look inward. What changes do you personally need to make in your attitudes and habits to be the sort of leader who can preside over a culture of ownership? In what ways do you need to build your own character strength so that when trouble hits, as you know it will, you'll always do the right thing instead of just doing the expedient thing?"

"Okay, that makes sense."

"Yes, but it wasn't just a rhetorical question. What's the answer? In what ways must you yourself change if you're going to be a leader who really does build a culture of ownership in your organization?"

Corey thought for a long moment. "In all honesty, I'm a bit of a control freak. When it comes to delegation, empowerment, and ownership, I can talk a good game, but it's everything I can do to keep myself from looking over people's shoulders after I've given them something to do."

"Which, of course, takes the wind right out of the empowerment sails."

"I know it's counterproductive," Corey said. "You can almost see the enthusiasm drain out of a person when you check up on them. Learning how to entrust someone with a responsibility, and then trusting them to fulfill it, is probably the biggest personal change I'll have to make." Corey read another note: *"The best way to build your own courage is to convince others of their courage."* He laughed and said, "It seems like whoever laid out all these sticky notes is reading my mind!"

"Maybe so," Walt replied. "Or maybe they're showing you the path to follow for building that culture of ownership. Shall we follow the yellow-note road?"

Corey stepped out onto the paper trail. "The longest journey begins with a single step. Let's go."

Corey read as many of the notes as he could as they stepped over them, every now and then stooping to pick one up that seemed especially meaningful. "Where do you suppose the yellow-note road is taking us, Walt?"

Walt smiled and winked. "The notes themselves are a clue. I believe we are about to meet William Lester McKnight. Have you heard of him?"

"No, can't say that I have. Is he the one who wrote all these notes?"

"No, but the paper upon which these notes are written is one part of the man's legacy. McKnight was CEO of the 3M Corporation from 1929 to 1966 and was responsible for creating the culture behind one of the world's most innovative companies. Jim Collins called McKnight the greatest CEO that almost no one has ever heard of. Oh, here we are."

Walt pointed to a small three-story building, and Corey followed him in that direction. As they walked, Walt said, "Post-it notes are the most famous example of how a culture of ownership has fostered innovation at 3M but are by no means the only one. Let's see how it all got started."

Walt and Corey were now standing in a small, poorly lit office. An older man in a brown suit sat behind a desk which, Corey noticed, had no telephone on it. Another, much younger, man sat in the chair in front of the desk. He was also wearing a suit. "That's Edgar Ober," Walt whispered, nodding toward the older man. "In

1911, he was 3M's CEO. And that," he said, nodding toward the younger man, "is William McKnight. Up until today, he's been the company's cost accountant." Walt was whispering, but it was obvious that neither man had any awareness of the fact that they were being observed. "Ober is trying to find someone to replace 3M's sales manager, who recently resigned."

Ober didn't waste any words. "McKnight, as you know, Pearse has left our company. I've been given a list of men who might be candidates for the sales manager position, but they are all from outside the company. It's my belief that a company should reward the hard work and loyalty of the men it already has before it looks outside, and you have been a loyal and hard-working member of the 3M family. So, McKnight, I want you to take on the sales manager job."

McKnight was clearly shocked by the offer. "Thank you, Mr. Ober, but I have no sales experience at all. I am completely unqualified for a job as a sales manager."

Ober leaned forward on his elbows and looked hard into McKnight's eyes. "When you and I met with Pearse about the quality problems we're having with our sandpaper—which is the reason our salesmen are having such a hard time selling it—you suggested that instead of trying to push an inferior product off on purchasing agents, our salesmen should go back into the shops and talk to the men who are actually using it. That's what I want you to do, McKnight. I want you to go into those shops and figure out what the workmen need. Then, we'll give it to them." Ober stood and reached his right hand across the desk. "McKnight, you're going to be the best salesman this company ever had."

McKnight shook Ober's hand and replied, "I'll do my best, sir."

Walt nudged Corey toward the door. "McKnight's best was about as good as any company could ever expect of a man. Let's jump ahead a bit and see how he's doing."

Walt led Corey through what appeared to be an industrial laboratory. He recognized William McKnight, clearly older and more confident than the young bookkeeper he'd seen protest that he was not qualified to be a sales manager. McKnight was walking with someone Corey surmised to be his assistant. He stopped in his tracks and stared across the room at a man who had his arms dunked up to the elbows in a tub of something that he was vigorously working. "Isn't that young Richard Drew?" McKnight asked his assistant.

"Why yes, I believe it is."

"Hmm. Didn't I tell him to stop wasting time on that nondrying tape project of his and go back to his lab assistant job?"

"Yes, sir, you did. I'll go see to it right now." The assistant turned to head off in Drew's direction, but McKnight grabbed his sleeve and pulled him back. "The best and hardest work is done in the spirit of adventure and challenge. Don't tell him we were here. Let's see what he comes up with."

"Do you know what young Mr. Drew came up with?" Walt asked. Corey shook his head no. "Masking tape, that's what. The guy ignored the direct order of the CEO and went on to invent masking tape! His creation launched 3M into adhesive products, which of course turned into one of the company's core businesses. Had McKnight held Drew 'accountable' for doing his assigned work in the lab, 3M probably never would have gotten into the adhesive business. There would be no Scotch tape on your desk, no Post-it notes posted on your computer screen."

"A sad world that would be," Corey said. "I can't imagine life without Post-it notes."

Walt laughed. "Who knows what wonderful things my Imagineers might have come up with had they had Post-it notes? What you've just seen was an early example of what became known at 3M as the Fifteen Percent Rule. Technical people are allowed—even encouraged—to spend fifteen percent of their time working on projects of their own choosing, regardless of whether those projects fall within the scope of their official job description. More than anything else, that's the reason that nearly one-third of 3M's sales come from products that didn't even exist four years ago."

"That sounds good in theory, Walt, but I also see how it could create chaos. I mean, if everyone can go off in any direction they choose, how do you maintain a coherent product family and marketing image?"

"Good questions. They do several things at 3M that minimize the risk of chaos. First, they don't just encourage people to develop new ideas and products; they also want them to share their knowledge and insights with others in the company. In fact, that's one of the key criteria for being selected for the Carlton Society, which is the highest form of peer recognition at 3M. Second, they are intensely market focused. McKnight used to tell his salespeople to look for smokestacks and then to talk to the people who worked beneath these stacks. Being market focused helps make sure that people are spending their time on projects that have real market potential. And third, when a new type of product does take off—the way Post-it notes did—the company will set up a new division to exploit and expand the product line. That way, the new product doesn't have to compete with or distract from existing product lines."

"You know, Walt, all that sounds great for a company that sells technology-intensive products, but I really don't see how it can apply in the hospitality business."

"Corey, as CEO, you are going to be surrounded by 'yes, but' men and women. Don't become one yourself. I want to show you something, but first, a question: Are you happy with the bedside lamps in your high-end hotel suites?"

"They're all right. Why do you ask?"

"All right? Is that the standard you strive for in your luxury rooms?"

Corey turned red and shook his head. "No, we want them to be deluxe in every way. The competition is fierce for executive travelers, and we need every advantage we can get—even if it's just having better bedside lamps."

"What do you think of this one?" Walt held up a beautiful wooden bedside lamp, but it was unlike anything Corey had ever seen before. Corey wasn't a woodworker, but even he could tell that great love had gone into the making of this lamp. It was a dark wood—cherry?—that had been polished to a soft luster. Instead of a traditional wraparound lampshade, this lamp featured a series of hammock-like baffles that were arranged around the underside of the light bulb. Corey instantly saw that this was a great solution to one of his own pet peeves: a light shining in his eyes when he was trying to read in bed. But the most remarkable part of this lamp was the wood base. It appeared to flow seamlessly into the lamp stem, but it was packed with electronic features: a touch-sensitive rheostat that regulated the light bulb, a luminescent clock that recognized voice commands for setting the alarm, and a docking station for an iPod that powered built-in stereo speakers. At the back of the lamp was a bank of electrical outlets connected to a built-in surge suppressor. Another of Corey's pet peeves was having to unplug the bedside clock in a hotel room so that he could plug in the extension cord he always carried in his overnight bag, since almost no hotel had enough outlets at the bedside for all of his gadgets.

"This is awesome, Walt! Where did you get it?"

"I'll show you," Walt replied. The two men were suddenly standing in what appeared to be a wood shop. A man in a surgical mask was working on a lamp just like the one that Walt had shown Corey. He was using a hammer and tiny chisel to chip out the space where the electronic components would go. After he'd laid the electronics in and fastened a velvet cover on the bottom, he turned the unit over and polished it with a soft cloth. He inserted a light bulb, checked the rheostat, and instructed the alarm clock to wake him up at 6:30 the next morning. Then he inserted an iPod into the cradle and turned it on, and installed the light shade to the strains of Frank Sinatra belting out "New York, New York." When everything was to his satisfaction, he took off the surgical mask and tossed it into a large trash bin next to the work bench.

Corey gasped when the man turned around. It was Brent Jacobs, the night-shift bookkeeper at the Surrey Inn and Suites hotel in Manhattan—the man he'd met at the airport earlier that morning, a time that now seemed to have been weeks ago.

10 | Lesson 8: Everyone Is a Volunteer

"Would you like to see where that beautiful lamp is going to find a home?" Walt asked Corey as Brent Jacobs' shop faded into the distance.

"Absolutely," Corey replied. "But please tell me it's not going into a VIP room at the Marriott or Ritz-Carlton."

"No, it's not going into a luxury hotel—quite to the contrary."

Corey heard the sound of hammers and drills in the distance. Gradually, the scene came into view. Dozens of people were building houses. The scene appeared to have been carefully choreographed—people carrying wood, pounding nails, scrutinizing blueprints, even delivering cups of hot coffee to the workers. "That's a Habitat for Humanity project," Walt said. "Those ten houses are going to be finished and occupied before the snow flies. And each master bedroom will be furnished with one of Brent Jacobs's beautiful high-tech lamps."

Corey shook his head. "Who would have known that our 'just a night-shift bookkeeper' would have such a talent?"

"*You* should have known, Corey. Someone at the company should know such things. How much more hidden talent is there at Owatt Hospitality—talent that could help you compete more effectively with the likes of Marriott and Ritz-Carlton? And how much more of a sense of ownership would these people have if you found a way to honor their talent by capitalizing on it?"

"That sounds good, Walt, but it's not realistic for us to know the hobbies and interests of every one of our employees."

"Oh, really? You spend a lot of time and money trying to learn about the hobbies and interests of your customers. Don't you think it's just as important to learn about your employees—perhaps even more important, since they are with you every day?"

Corey nodded, deep in thought as he watched people working on the Habitat homes. "You're right, Walt. If we could find a way to help people engage in their work by sharing their strengths and passions, we would have a stronger company, and they would have more rewarding work. Look at how hard those people are working—and they're volunteering their time!"

Walt laughed. "No one ever walked off the job at a Habitat for Humanity construction project in a pay dispute! Peter Drucker wrote that organizations should treat their employees as if they were all volunteers, because they are. They're getting paid while they're on the job, of course, but in today's world they all have other options. There's a lot to be learned from studying how the best volunteer organizations recruit and keep their best volunteers."

Corey nodded thoughtfully. "Like the independent beauty consultants of Mary Kay and the franchisees of McDonald's—they are part of the team, even though they're not being paid by the organization. I wonder how Brent got involved with Habitat for Humanity."

"Let's find out," Walt replied. The two men were suddenly standing at the back of an auditorium. There were about a hundred people sitting in folding chairs. The speaker at the podium was tall and lean and obviously passionate about his message. "That's Millard Fuller," Walt said, "the man who founded Habitat for Humanity. Do you recognize the guy in the back row with the baseball cap?" Corey nodded—it was a younger Brent Jacobs with his arms folded and the same skeptical look on his face that he'd been wearing in their airport conversation that morning. Corey tuned in to Fuller's speech:

"At Habitat for Humanity, we follow several basic principles. We depend on volunteers: volunteers who care about their fellow human beings in need; volunteers who give their money, their time, and their God-given talents. These volunteers form partnerships with each other, with churches, with other organizations, and with people in need."

Corey noticed that Jacobs had lifted his chin and seemed to be listening more carefully. Fuller continued:

"This partnership disregards social status, gender, skin color, cultural differences, and faith differences. We call this 'the theology of the hammer.' The theology of the hammer brings together all kinds of people, all kinds of organizations, all kinds of churches and religious traditions, and all kinds of institutions to build and renovate houses with and for needy families."

Corey shifted his attention back and forth between Brent Jacobs and Millard Fuller. He thought of his favorite definition of selling: the transference of belief from one person to another. Jacobs was now leaning forward, hands on knees, listening intently. Corey sensed that a sale was being made. Fuller built to his conclusion:

"We are a Christian organization, but we are not exclusive and not doctrinal. Our desire is to put faith and love to work; to make a difference; to change things and change people for the better. Please come join us—help us make the world a better place. I'd be happy to answer any questions."

Brent Jacobs slowly raised his hand, and Fuller called on him. "Do you need any custom furniture for these houses?" Fuller looked like a kid who'd been offered the entire basket of candy while out trick-or-treating and invited Jacobs to speak with him at the front of the room. Corey saw them shaking hands as the scene faded.

"That was almost fifteen years ago," Walt said to Corey, "and Brent has been a devoted Habitat volunteer ever since. It seems like he's a lot more motivated by his volunteer work than he is by his job, doesn't it?"

"Yes, yes it does. So, what do you suggest, Walt?"

"In his book *Drive,* Daniel Pink says that most modern organizations have the motivation equation all wrong. They're still into the carrot-and-stick approach of rewards and punishment. But the best that sort of an accountability-oriented approach can do is assure people's compliance with rules and procedures. Pink says that if you really want people to be engaged in their work, there must be three conditions—each of which is present when someone volunteers their time to build a Habitat for Humanity house. The first element, he says, is autonomy. Nobody likes to have Big Brother looking over his or her shoulder. Brent doesn't have a boss breathing down his neck when he's working in his woodshop, building lamps for Habitat."

Walt and Corey were now back at the site where the new Habitat for Humanity houses were going up. Walt continued: "The second essential driver of motivation, Pink says, is mastery. People must feel like they're continuously enhancing their skills and knowledge—which they will if there's a real culture of ownership. Do you see the way those master carpenters are teaching the beginners how to set a window? How would you like to see that sort of expression on the face of an Owatt housekeeper who's being shown a better way to strip and wax a floor?" Corey laughed and held up two thumbs.

Walt stretched the fingers of his right hand as though he longed to walk over to the worksite and grab a hammer himself. "Those people aren't just pounding nails and hauling wood; they have a purpose. That's the third element of motivation that Pink describes and at which Millard Fuller was such a genius: imputing a sense of greater purpose into what otherwise would have been mundane work. Motivating people with autonomy, mastery, and purpose is about as good a definition of real leadership as you will find."

Corey kicked a stone in the general direction of the building project. "Creating autonomy, mastery, and purpose is going to be a challenge, as most of our people have relatively unskilled jobs like cleaning hotel rooms and waiting tables."

"I can appreciate that," Walt said. "We had many of the same issues at Disneyland. But you have to find the motivational hot buttons that cause people to take ownership for their work. Let's look at your hotel housekeepers. I doubt very many of them come to work every day with their top goal being to make the boss look good. Am I right?"

"Yeah," Corey replied with a laugh, "and that's probably the understatement of the year."

"Zig Ziglar says that we all listen to the same radio station: WIIFM, or 'What's in It for Me?' So, what's in it for the house-keeper to take pride of ownership in the work?" Before Corey could answer, Walt went on: "Have you read *The Dream Manager* by Matthew Kelly?" Corey shook his head indicating that he had not, and silently wondered how it was that Walt Disney was able to keep up on books that had been published since he died. "Well," Walt said, "it's a fictional story with a real-world message. The American Dream, as Kelly describes in his story, is to own your own home. How many of the people who work in housekeeping for Owatt Hospitality own their own homes?

"I would say probably not very many."

"And what if you took Kelly's advice and hired a 'dream manager' to help some of these people fulfill their dreams of someday owning their own homes?"

Corey started to say something, then held his tongue. "My 'yes, but' man was about to come out with all the reasons that wouldn't work," he finally said. "But it's something worth considering."

"Here's something else worth considering," Walt said. "Habitat for Humanity doesn't just give houses to people; it makes them invest sweat equity. The average is five hundred hours. Because they have invested a part of themselves in the building of their houses, people are much more likely to keep them up. There's a more general lesson there: A culture of ownership creates higher expectations for the people who work there. Southwest Airlines has an exemplary ownership culture. It also has by far the highest productivity in the airline industry."

Corey watched as the crew members who had been carrying lumber from trucks to the houses took a break. They were clearly exhausted, but everyone was smiling and laughing. "You know, Walt," he said, "if we could somehow bottle that spirit, we'd have an unstoppable organization. Imagine a workplace where at the end of the day, people went home physically tired because they've been putting everything into their work but emotionally and spiritually uplifted because of everything they've gotten out of their work."

"Yep," Walt continued, "attitude really is everything. You know that some of these Habitat for Humanity volunteers don't work nearly as hard at their day jobs as they're working right now for no pay, but they complain a lot more about how hard they have to work at those day jobs. That's going to be a big part of your challenge, Corey. How do you make it rewarding to clean a hotel room? Or rather, how do you make it rewarding to clean a hotel room when it's the twelfth room you've cleaned that morning?"

"I'm not sure that's really possible, Walt. It's hard to give a housekeeper a sense of ownership for cleaning a room."

Walt cocked his head slightly, clearly unhappy with Corey's suggestion that something was not possible. "How about letting them select the artwork for *their* rooms—the rooms they clean every day?"

Corey looked skeptical—his "yes but" man was getting the upper hand on this one, and this time Corey thought he probably should. "We want our hotels to have a certain image, to make our guests feel like they are in a home away from home. They don't want to see pictures of a housekeeper's children—or pictures painted by their children that belong on the fridge at home, not on the wall of a classy hotel."

Walt laughed and shook his head. "There you go again, Corey. How can you make your housekeepers feel like owners when you yourself don't think you can trust them to act like owners. Today, some of the most successful Disney hotels do exactly that—let housekeepers choose artwork for *their* rooms. And if they're putting up their kids' fridge-paintings, there have certainly been no complaints."

Corey laughed as he visualized his mental "yes but" man slinking off to a corner of his mind. "Well, I suppose it couldn't hurt to try it out at one of our hotels, see how it works, then let it grow from there. Maybe we'll start with Brent's place."

Walt nodded approvingly. "It's a paradox: The more you appreciate that people are really volunteers, the more important it is that you give them a strong sense of job security. Every one of the leaders we've visited today did that, and it's a principle that I followed myself. I never fired anyone who was honestly trying to do their job. And almost no one who started with us at Disney Studio ever left, voluntarily or otherwise. We had a lot of people who were on our payroll their entire working lives. Too many managers today think of people as assets rather than as resources. Accountants depreciate assets and then write them off. Real leaders know that the futures of their businesses depend upon investing in people as resources, not writing off people as assets."

Corey rubbed his cheeks and frowned. "There's been a lot of discussion at the board and management levels about whether we should have a layoff at Owatt. I'm concerned that the cost could outweigh any benefit. The research I've seen suggests that layoffs aren't usually a very good solution if you're trying to create a more competitive company."

Walt nodded vigorously. "A layoff almost always reflects a failure of leadership. You know, we share one another's fates, and leaders are responsible for creating the circumstances that allow people to be successful. Sometimes, there's no alternative, but it should always be a last resort. Of course, creating those circumstances that allow you to provide job security depends upon people fulfilling their part of the bargain by bringing their A-game to work every day."

"I'm afraid that not everyone at Owatt does bring their A-game to work every day," Corey said. "And that's something I'm going to have to work on."

"One more thing," Walt said, nodding his approval. "You've got to be in it for the long haul. It took Habitat for Humanity fifteen years to build their first ten thousand homes. It only took another two years to build the second ten thousand homes and only fourteen months to build the third ten thousand."

"That reminds me of the story of John Wooden, the legendary UCLA basketball coach," Corey replied. "He was there for sixteen years before he won his first national championship. Then he won ten of the next twelve. What if the school had given up on him after fifteen years? They would have gone back to Go without their two hundred dollars and started all over again."

Walt looked off into the distance, and Corey imagined that he was reminiscing about all the times in his long career that he must have been tempted to quit, to get a real job—and how glad he was that he never did. "Young man," Walt said with a touch of sadness in his voice, "you are about to begin on a magnificent journey. Make sure that you take a lot of people with you."

11 | The Four Essential Elements of a Culture of Ownership

"We're here." Corey felt a gentle tap on his knee and awoke with a start. "Sorry to wake you, Mr. Whitaker, but we're at the bank building." Jerry the limo driver was holding the door open, and the sounds of a New York City morning filled the air.

"Where's Walt?" Corey rubbed his eyes and looked at the other empty seats in the limo.

"Where's who?" Jerry cocked his head inquisitively.

"Nothing. It was a dream." Corey grabbed his briefcase and stepped out onto the sidewalk. He looked up at the bank's running news banner: European stock markets had opened the day higher, elections had again been postponed in Iraq, and it was 7:45 in the morning. Fifteen minutes to go until his meeting with the bankers. Corey pulled out his cell phone and dialed his office. He told his secretary that he'd be staying an extra day in New York City and asked her to make a reservation that evening for him at the Surrey Park Inn and Suites. He bought a cup of coffee and a donut from a sidewalk vendor and listened to the music of the streets while he organized his thoughts.

When he'd finished his donut, Corey placed a second call. "Hi Monika, this is Corey Whitaker from Owatt Hospitality . . . Fine, thanks, and you? . . . Is Mr. Williamson in? . . . Great. Tell him that I have an answer for him." Corey smiled at how much more quickly his phone calls were answered now that he had the CEO title. "Doug, I've changed my mind. If the offer is still on the table, I accept . . . No, that won't be a problem; my board will go along with it . . . Excellent. I'll stop by this afternoon to shake hands on the deal. Then we can turn it over to the lawyers and the bean counters . . . Super. I'll be by about 4:30."

At five minutes before the hour, Corey walked into the bank's executive offices and was directed to the boardroom. He recognized Danielle Hoover as the vice president who managed Owatt's loan portfolio. She introduced him to the four other people in the room, including William Gordon, the executive vice president Corey had heard his predecessor refer to as "Bone Crusher." It was Gordon who called the meeting to order. "First of all, on behalf of the bank and all of our officers, let me congratulate you on being offered the CEO position and give you my condolences for having accepted it." He looked around the room with a knowing smile, and as if on cue each of the vice presidents smiled and nodded back. "So, let's talk about what you're going to do during your first hundred days on the job."

Corey was about to make his introductory comments when Gordon interrupted. "Before you do, just so we are all clear about what's going on, let's get it out on the table that you are technically in violation of bond covenants. In particular, your debt-to-equity and liquidity ratios are out of line—substantially out of line. Technically speaking, you could already be in default."

Corey opened his portfolio and looked at the first page of his prepared remarks. "That's true, but if you look a little closer—"

Gordon cut him off with a wave of the hand. "Your first challenge as CEO will, of course, be an intensive campaign of cost reduction. Why don't we begin with that? Tell us what your plans are."

Corey's laptop was loaded with the PowerPoint presentation he'd put together with his leadership team. It spelled out what they might do to cut costs: They could close or sell 23 unprofitable properties, lay off 53 people from the headquarters staff, impose an across-the-board 10 percent staffing reduction at their remaining 382 properties, and freeze all salaries except for those of managers, who could take a 10 percent pay cut. "Draconian" was the team's consensus term for the plan, but it was the only way they could get back on track financially without selling assets. *Draconian*—the word echoed in Corey's mind—*as in the work of Dracula.* Corey had been amazed at how the management team had come together working on this plan. Their meetings had gone late into the evenings and been punctuated by anger, arguments, and tears. But in the end, they had come together, and each pledged their support to do whatever had to be done to make it work.

Except that it wouldn't really work. As the term "draconian" implied, Corey feared that these cutbacks would suck the life's blood out of his organization. He had a choice to make, and he'd made it 15 minutes ago. They would sell assets.

"Mr. Whitaker?" Bill Gordon was showing his impatience.

Corey left the laptop in his briefcase lying on the floor and closed up his portfolio. Then, he leaned forward on his elbows and looked individually at each person in the room, finally fixing his eyes upon Gordon. "You asked if we have a plan to cut expenses, and the answer is that yes, we do. It's all laid out on a PowerPoint presentation in my briefcase. I'll be happy to share it with you if you'd like to see it. But you will have to understand that it's only a contingency plan—a last resort if our primary plan does not work. It's our primary plan I would like to share with you this morning." Corey leaned back in his chair and tried to look calm and confident, but inside, he was in a panic. He was about to take a huge risk: a risk that was based upon—what? A dream he'd had riding in a limo from the airport? And a commitment that he'd made only 15 minutes ago?

"I think you all know that I've spent most of my career at Owatt. I started as an assistant restaurant manager in Minneapolis twenty-five years ago and have worked in almost every division since. So, I remember the glory days, back when we were an annual fixture on the *Fortune* magazine roster of the world's most admired companies and when revenues and profits were consistently growing in double digits. Unfortunately, we let it go to our heads. We got complacent. We were able to coast for a while, but eventually it all caught up to us, and we started losing money. That's when the bean counters took charge, and we got accountability on steroids. But the price was that we lost something vital—something precious. We lost the enthusiasm and the creativity that made Owatt the great company it once was."

"Do we really need this history lesson?" Gordon asked. "We're all familiar with what your problems have been."

"Yes, I think it's important to set the stage. You see, the account-ability pendulum has swung much too far toward the left brain. We've become so obsessed with counting beans that we forgot our future success depends upon planting beans. What had been a culture that encouraged entrepreneurial thinking gradually mor-phed into one where people were more concerned with covering their tracks than they were with blazing new trails. Though no one would have admitted it publicly, we went from being a company that was determined to win to one where we've been playing to not lose." Corey tapped the tabletop with his fingertip for empha-sis. "We're going to go back to our roots, remember who we are, and start playing to win again. That's my plan."

Gordon rapped the table with his pen. "We still have this little problem: You are noncompliant with your loan covenants, and we are concerned about your ability to make payments going forward. Frankly, Mr. Whitaker, we were expecting to hear your plans for tightening your belt, not for putting on weight." This comment earned another round of laughter from his colleagues. "And where do you expect to find capital for all of this entrepreneurial zeal?"

"We're going to sell an asset."

"You're going to sell *an* asset?"

"That's right. We're going to sell an asset. We're going to sell the Desert Plum Casino."

"Are you crazy?" It was Danielle Hoover who asked, obviously shocked by this news. "The Desert Plum has been your cash cow for the past five years."

"I know," Corey replied, "but we think this is the right time to get out of the casino business, for several reasons. First, it's really not our core strength, and it diverts a lot of management attention from those areas that are core strengths. Second, our market research department has looked at national polling data and forecasts a strong return to traditional values in the coming years; we believe that's going to be very bad news for the gambling business, and we want to get out of it before the roof caves in, which it almost certainly will do given the gross overcapacity in the industry. Finally, I'm sure Cecil Owatt has been rolling over in his grave ever since we bought the Desert Plum six years ago. He never would have countenanced us getting involved in the gambling business. It's time for us to take our capital gains and let Mr. Owatt rest in peace."

Corey looked around the room; the bankers seemed to be in a state of silent shock, so he continued. "The cash we bring in from selling the casino will help us strengthen our balance sheet and give us the opportunity to refocus the business. My first priority as CEO will be to build a stronger cultural foundation. You've heard the saying that 'culture eats strategy for lunch.' We believe that's a true statement. For the past six years, we've followed a strategy of diversification, including our foray into the gambling business. This year, we're going to work as hard on building a culture of ownership as we have been working on increasing the number of properties we own." Corey stood up. "Is it okay if I draw on the whiteboard?" Gordon nodded, and Corey picked up a marker pen. "Our leadership group has identified four essential characteristics for building a culture of ownership—a culture where people think and act like partners in the enterprise and not just hired hands renting a spot on the organization chart. The first and most important of these four is commitment." Corey printed the words in big block letters on the whiteboard:

Commitment: To Values, Vision, and Mission

He tapped the whiteboard with the marker. "When I was looking through old files in the CEO office, I came across something I hadn't seen for many years. Shortly after Cecil Owatt started our company, he put together a statement of guiding values, operating principles, and behavioral expectations. That statement should really define who we are—what we stand for and what we won't stand for. And as the old country song says, 'If you don't stand for something, you'll fall for anything.' I don't think it's a coincidence that it was shortly after the values plaques we had up on the walls got replaced with expensive artwork that we started to get into trouble. Over the next several months, I am personally going to lead our management group through workshops on those values, principles, and expectations. We'll make any changes that are necessary to make it current, then ask everyone to sign a statement of commitment."

"And if they don't sign?" It was Robbie Johansen asking, who'd been introduced as the bank's newest vice president.

"They'll be invited to go work for one of our competitors. And I will personally schedule their farewell party for the next day." Robbie raised his eyebrows and gave the slightest nod of approval. Corey continued. "Then, we're going to expect every manager to conduct the same training for each and every one of their employees, and so on down throughout the organization."

Corey took off his jacket and draped it across the back of his chair, then went back to the whiteboard. "The second essential characteristic of a culture of ownership is employee engagement. You've probably seen Gallup survey results showing that only about one-quarter of workers in the typical company are truly engaged in their work. The rest are either not engaged and just going through the motions, zombies enduring their days on autopilot, or they are aggressively disengaged, vampires sucking the life out of their work unit and their co-workers. Those are the ones who see management, and not marketplace competitors, as the enemy." Corey wrote on the board:

Engagement: With Customers, with Coworkers, with the Work Itself

"Jeff Pfeffer is a professor at the Stanford Graduate School of Business, which is where I got my MBA. In one of his books, he tells the story of a time back in the early eighties when the Mazda car company ran into financial trouble. As an alternative to laying people off, they took workers from the factory floor, put them through a crash course on selling techniques, gave them briefcases full of brochures, and sent them door-to-door selling cars. That year, all ten of the company's top salespeople were factory workers. It saved the company."

"So, are you going to send your hotel housekeepers door-to-door selling nights in deluxe suites?" Corey recognized John Bender, who he'd been warned would be most aggressive about wanting the company to reduce expenses.

"Actually, we're going to do something very similar. We're calling it 'Invite a Friend to Dinner.' Every associate will receive a supply of coupons for ten percent off meals in our restaurants. Every coupon will have their employee number on it. For every five coupons that are turned in, we will award that associate one share of Owatt stock. Of course, not everyone will take us up on it at first, but we think it will do a lot to engage people in their work and in our company. First, they are directly rewarded by receiving a share of stock; second, they are rewarded every time our stock price increases."

The bankers in the room all looked skeptical, but no one interrupted, so Corey continued. "The third essential characteristic of a culture of ownership is passion. Bill Bennett said there are no menial jobs, only menial attitudes, and we couldn't agree more." Corey wrote on the board:

Passion: Enthusiasm for the Work and Fellowship in the Workplace

"Especially in a service business like ours, passionate people are a great competitive advantage. One of the guiding values Cecil Owatt laid out was the importance of having fun at work. In our rush to hold people accountable, we've forgotten how to have fun; and yet, especially in the restaurant business, our customer surveys tell us that people don't become raving fans because of the food and the service but rather because they had fun. We know the only way our customers will have fun is if our associates are having fun. Furthermore, in a high-turnover business like ours, making sure people are having fun is the ultimate retention strategy."

Corey glanced at the clock on the wall and saw that he had only 10 minutes left. "The fourth essential characteristic of a culture of ownership is pride." Corey wrote on the whiteboard one last time:

Pride: In the Organization, the Job, and Themselves

"Over the past several years, we've made some decisions that were penny-wise and pound-foolish. At the top of that list of shortsighted decisions are the reductions we've made in our commitment to training. The best way to make sure people are proud of their work is to assure competence and motivation through training. We are recommitting ourselves to having the best-trained people in the industry. We're also going to invest in sharp new uniforms that have a contemporary feel to them. It's hard to be proud of your job when you're wearing a costume that screams 'just a janitor' or 'just a busboy.' And we're going to give every associate their own personal business cards. Mary Kay Ash told her beauty consultants to imagine that everyone they met wore a sign saying 'Make Me Feel Important.' We are once again going to make MMFI part of our corporate culture, beginning with our own people."

Corey set the marker pen back in the tray. "That's just some of what we intend to do. In the months to come, we're going to get a lot more people involved in the planning and implementation process. I'll be happy to send you a copy of our plan once it's been finalized. Are there any questions?"

After a long silence Bill Gordon said, "Frankly, Corey, this is a breath of fresh air that we've waited a long time to feel. My only concern is your planned sale of the Desert Plum Casino. I think it's way underpriced at just six hundred forty million. Why don't you let us help you negotiate a better deal?"

Corey smiled as he thought of Ray Kroc shaking hands with Chuck the bread man. "Thanks, Bill, but the deal is already done."

12 | It Takes Courage and Strength of Character to Be a Culture Leader

It was ten o'clock on a Friday night at the end of Corey's first full month in the CEO's office. Still shaken from the board meeting the night before, he stood at his window, looking at the city lights below. He'd known he had the votes to sustain his decision to sell the Desert Plum Casino, but he had never expected the meeting to be so contentious or the vote to be so close. Darby O'Keefe, who had been the most vocal proponent of getting into the casino business in the first place, made no bones of the fact that he thought Corey's emphasis on corporate culture was a waste of time and that his one and only responsibility was maximizing return to the shareholders. That was no surprise to Corey; what *was* a surprise was that O'Keefe had the support of a significant minority of board members.

Corey had been on the road almost nonstop since becoming CEO. He'd spoken with hundreds of Owatt employees, taking copious notes. And he felt like he had been beaten up pretty badly. He knew the previous CEO was not exactly a people-person but was still shocked at the level of antagonism and ill will he had created. "I should have insisted on combat pay when I negotiated for this job," he said to himself with a laugh.

"At least you've kept your sense of humor. The day you can no longer laugh at your troubles is the day that you really are in trouble." Corey turned around with a start and was astonished to see Walt Disney sitting in the chair by the window, one leg crossed over the other, wearing his trademark smile. "If you stop laughing, you'll start taking yourself too seriously. I believe that sort of self-absorption gets more CEOs into trouble than any other single cause."

Corey stood there with his mouth open for a few seconds and then was finally able to speak. "So, it wasn't just a dream, was it? I never really thought it was."

"As I told you, Corey, reality is a far more malleable concept than we left-brained westerners care to acknowledge. And the difference between dreaming and waking is more subtle than we imagine. But I'm afraid this will be my last visit, so we had better get to work. Your watch won't stop this time, and we have some important things to cover."

Corey picked up a pen and pad from his desk and walked over to the chair facing Walt. "I think it's going to be quite a while before I'm able to work on a book, but at least I'm taking your advice and writing things down so that I'll have lots of raw material to work with when the time comes. Although after the board meeting yesterday, the option of a writing career might come up a lot sooner than I thought it would."

"Look, Corey, you should be thankful that this little fight happened as quickly as it did. Your board is going to test you, your employees are going to test you, and your competitors are going to test you. Get used to it. These challenges are not only going to test your character, but they are also going to mold it. You're going to need courage. Remember what that yellow note you picked up from the road said: *'Fear is a reaction; courage is a decision.'* Courage is the main quality of leadership—courage to initiate something and determination keep it going. The best leaders have a pioneering spirit—an adventurous spirit; they have the courage to blaze new trails in this incredible land of opportunity. Getting your company out of the gambling business might not have been the best business decision, but it was the right thing to do for deeper reasons: being true to your values."

"So, what do you think I should do now, Walt?"

Walt folded his hands on his knee and thought for a moment. "Back in the darkest days of the Great Depression, Mickey Mouse saved our company—literally. Licensing and merchandising got us out of a financial hole and gave us a bit of a cushion. The first thing I did when I had a little extra cash was set up an in-house school for our artists. People thought I was crazy—that is, until they started to see how much better our artists got when we got serious about training. Every one of the companies you and I visited during our little adventure takes training very seriously. You should, as well. And ignore the naysayers on your board; an investment in your people is the best investment you could possibly make."

Walt sighed nostalgically, and Corey sensed that he was thinking about dreams he hadn't had the time to fulfill. "You've also got to loosen the death grip the previous management had on this place. People are so afraid of failing that they won't take risks, and we both know that is the greatest formula of all for ultimate failure. You've got a lot of people like Brent Jacobs in this organization; you need to give them wings and let them fly."

Walt's image flickered slightly, and Corey knew it wouldn't be much longer before he departed. "You're saving the hardest for last, aren't you, Walt?"

Walt chuckled and said, "You are very perceptive. And you are correct. Your biggest challenge will be to redefine your business. Right now, you're giving lots of paying customers a soft bed and a hot meal. That's fine as far as it goes, but it has no magic to stir the soul. Think of the companies we visited. Their founding leaders had a mission that transcends mere business: They were out to change the world. How are you going to change the world?"

"But Walt," Corey protested, "we *are* in the hotel and restaurant business. That's what we do—give people soft beds and hot meals. Turning our hotels into homeless shelters might be a nice thing to do, but it would quickly bankrupt our company."

"I'm not suggesting that you turn your hotels into homeless shelters. But even there, I will challenge the notion that there's nothing you can do. As I'm sure you know, hotel occupancy and homelessness are countercyclical. When the economy is bad, fewer people travel, and more people lose their homes. What would be wrong with sectioning off rooms that are empty anyway as a place where people who are down on their luck can get a good night of sleep and a hot shower?"

Corey sat in silence and shook his head. "I can see it now—the reaction of Darby O'Keefe and his little clique—when I tell them we're going to set up a homeless shelter on a vacant floor of the Surrey Park Inn and Suites."

Walt shook his head. His image was getting faint, and his voice was starting to crackle. "I'm not suggesting that, though I think you might be surprised at the sort of support you would get—even, eventually, from Darby O'Keefe. You need to dream big, Corey. There was a reason Tom Watson renamed his company International Business Machines instead of Brooklyn Business Machines. There was a reason Mary Kay Ash told her independent beauty consultants they could prioritize their lives with God first, family second, and career last. There was a reason Ray Kroc refused to take a paycheck for eight years while he helped his franchisees get rich. There was a reason Millard Fuller set as the goal for Habitat for Humanity the eradication of poverty housing everywhere on the face of the earth, not just in Georgia. And there was a reason I would settle for nothing less than making Disneyland the happiest place on earth. Remember General Robert Wood Johnson?" Corey nodded. "He once said, 'Why be unreasonable when, with a little more effort, you can be impossible?' That is great advice, Corey. Set impossible goals, then achieve them. If you can dream it, you can do it."

Walt's image was now barely more than a vapor, his voice slightly more than a whisper. "Take the advice of Steve Jobs—who, I understand, is now the biggest stockholder in my company, though it *is* still my company—when he spoke at the business school of your alma mater, Stanford: He told the graduates that they should stay hungry and foolish, be willing to take risks, and settle for nothing less than being insanely great. That's great advice, Corey. And I'll add this: don't ever let anyone else stop you—especially not you."

13 | A Culture of Ownership Is a Bilateral Relationship

Corey had called an urgent meeting of his management team for the day he returned from New York—the day after the meeting with the bank. As he expected, his decision to get Owatt out of the gambling business had generated heated discussion. And he'd not been surprised when several days later, Kevin Manley, the vice president who was responsible for the Las Vegas operations, had submitted his resignation. The announcement of his decision to launch a new Cecil Owatt Fellows program, and his granting of the first fellowship to Brent Jacobs, had been better received. Cecil's Fellows, as they would be called, were encouraged to spend one day a week of paid time working on projects that had the potential to launch new businesses for Owatt. Corey already had a vision of Brent being Owatt's version of Art Fry, the man who created the Post-it note for 3M.

During their little adventure together, Corey and Walt had often talked about paradox. Now, he smiled at the paradox that the first steps toward building a culture of ownership had to be unilateral decisions on his part. A committee would never have agreed to sell the Desert Plum, and the Cecil Owatt Fellows program was so far out of the box for what had become a very conservative company that no committee would have even thought of it. He would, on occasion, have to make more tough decisions during his tenure as CEO—the way that James Burke had to insist upon the Tylenol recall and that Mary Kay determined to regain her independence by taking her company private.

But even more, his job would be to make sure that there was leadership in every corner of Owatt, not just in the corner office. He'd been reading more about how McDonald's built mutually empowering relationships with its franchisees and suppliers, about the methods people like Millard Fuller used to inspire volunteers to put heart and soul as well as hands into tough jobs, and about how the other leaders to whom he'd been introduced by Walt created the sort of culture that encouraged people to take real ownership for the work.

Most of all, he'd been studying the life and work of Walt Disney himself. Now, he picked up a dog-eared copy of a Disney biography that was at the top of a pile of books on his desk, turned to a page marked by a yellow Post-it note, and read this quote from Walt: "I feel there is no door which, with the kind of talent we have in our organization, could not be opened, and we hope we can continue to unlock these barriers as long as we are in the business of bringing a happy note into people's lives." Corey read that line several times; then he turned to his computer. He had an important letter to write.

An Open Letter to the People of Owatt Hospitality

Dear Colleagues:

Since taking the position of CEO six months ago, I've had the privilege of speaking with many of you, and I hope I'll have the opportunity to meet with everyone before too very long. I've been deeply touched by many of the stories I've heard. We're going to be collecting our stories and posting them on our web site. Today, I'd like to share one of these stories with you.

Several months ago, our management team considered a proposal from Mari Colladay, who is manager of the Owatt Plaza Hotel here in Baltimore, to sponsor a career day for homeless people in our community, some of whom are victims of the recent economic downturn. We considered her proposal carefully, then turned it down. Well, Mari just assumed that her proposal was rejected because she wasn't thinking big enough. So, on her own, she started the Baltimore Owatt Career Center for people who are down on their luck. There are selection criteria, and there are rules that must be followed by participants, but each month, Mari is selecting fifteen homeless people and helping them to get back on their feet. She has turned a section of one floor of her hotel—an area that is almost always unoccupied—into a dormitory. Students have one month in this safe haven to learn new skills and make appointments for job interviews.

I want you to know that had Mari come back to us with that idea, that bigger dream of hers, we would not have approved it. And that would have been a big mistake on our part. Thankfully, Mari did not come back to us for approval; her attitude was to "proceed until apprehended." Mari has now had two groups go through her program. No one has broken so much as a coffee cup, and Mari tells me that the people she calls "her students" are being very respectful to the staff. The best part is that four of her students have already found jobs.

I tell you this story for several reasons. The first is to introduce you to Tori Ridgeway and Paul Bonner, two graduates of Mari's program who are now working in the Owatt Environmental Services Department. The second is to announce that we will be expanding the Owatt Career Center to other locations. This will be done in a careful and planned way, and I'm pleased to tell you that Mari Colladay has been promoted to an assistant vice president position, where she will oversee this new program.

Finally, I'm sharing this story with you because I think it reflects who we really want to be. Our founder, Cecil Owatt, was a great businessman, but he was also a generous and big-hearted humanitarian. As your CEO, I am committed to restoring our business to its former greatness but also to reminding us all that we're not in business just to fill hotel-room beds and restaurant seats but also to make our corner of the world a better place.

I'm going to need your help—all of you. In our management meetings, we've been talking about building a culture of ownership here at Owatt Hospitality. We are committed to doing that. But a culture of ownership is a two-way street. We need your ideas; we need your enthusiasm. We need you to bring your best game to work every day. We need you to treat our resources as you would your own and to treat our guests as you would members of your own family. Tell us what you would do if you owned Owatt Hospitality—because in some very important ways, you already do.

Walt Disney once said that 'if you can dream it, you can do it.' Over the past several years, this company has stopped dreaming because we've been trying so hard to survive. We are going to start dreaming again. And we are going to start doing again. We are going to reignite the spirit that this company once had. It's going to be an exciting ride. Will you join us?

Very Best Wishes,
Corey Whitaker

Afterword

The knot on the cover of this book is a Carrick bend. It's a figure-8 knot, thus reflecting the eight essential lessons for building a culture of ownership that are described in this book. But the knot itself is also a beautiful metaphor for the book's main theme. A Carrick bend is used to securely bind two ropes together as in the way that a culture of ownership creates intense bonds of loyalty between organizations and the people who work there. It is a very stable binding that is also aesthetically beautiful in the manner of the great companies whose founding leaders you've met in this book. You might have seen it in macramé artwork without having recognized it as a metaphor for a great organization!

Appendix 1
Blueprinting the Invisible Architecture

When someone (customer, patient, visitor, prospective employee) first walks into your organization, their initial impression will be created by the physical surroundings. They will have a very different impression if you're located in a fancy new office building with a fountain in the lobby than if you're located in a rehabilitated warehouse down at dockside. Knowing this, you've doubtless put a lot of thought into the design and furnishing of your space, probably with professional help to make sure you get the details just right.

But lasting impressions aren't created by things that can be seen by the eye, are they? Rather, they're created by the unseen qualities that spark emotional reactions. This emotionality is vital to the future of every business, including that of your organization. Most business leaders don't put the same detailed thought that they invest in physical design into the design of this invisible architecture. If you take the time, though, it can be one of the best investments you'll ever make.

There are three interrelated dimensions of the architecture which can be seen only with the heart and not with the eyes: core values, corporate culture, and emotional environment.

Core values: Most organizations have (or should have) a statement of values, but very few have effectively utilized their commitment to these values as a resource for recruiting and retaining great people and competing for loyal customers.

Corporate culture: Culture is to the organization what character and personality are to the individual. Culture is the only sustainable source of competitive advantage, because it is the one thing that no competitor can copy or steal. Culture is defined by a very small number of overarching themes, which are then woven into all of the different subcultures throughout the organization.

Emotional environment: This is the emotional climate of the work unit—what it feels like to work in each part of the organization. Workplace environment is the most important determinant of whether people feel engaged in the work itself or are simply going through the motions for a paycheck. Unfortunately, a small number of negative people can poison a workplace the way one or two smokers quickly fill a room with toxic cigarette smoke.

Each of these elements of the invisible architecture of your organization (or your part of the organization) is amenable to your influence. In fact, influencing these three dimensions of the invisible architecture is perhaps the most important of all leadership responsibilities. If you are a parent, with a bit of thought you can apply many of these concepts and principles at home. Remember this important point: You do not have to be the CEO in order to influence the invisible architecture of your organization. Quite to the contrary, unlike the physical facility, in which design and construction is delegated to a small and specialized crew, the invisible architecture is influenced by each of us as we go about our daily business.

Appendix 2
The
Self-Empowerment
Pledge

Would you invest 365 minutes over the next year to dramatically improve the quality of your life? One minute per day. Would you give up one television commercial and instead use that minute to invest yourself with personal power?

The cubicles of corporate America are filled with people waiting to be empowered, complaining that nobody ever empowers them, yet who are scared to death that someone might actually expect them to act as if they were empowered. In truth, no one can empower you but you. The only genuine empowerment is self-empowerment. Once you empower yourself, though, nobody can take that power away. Empowerment is a state of mind—not part of a job description, a set of delegated tasks, or the latest management program brought in by the boss.

The Self-Empowerment Pledge includes seven simple promises that will change your life. Read these seven promises, then ask yourself this question: *If I were to act upon these promises, would I be in a better place—personally, professionally, financially, and spiritually—than where my current life trajectory is taking me?* If you're honest, the answer will be absolutely yes. The promises themselves are simple, but keeping them will require desire and determination. Fortunately, you don't have to do it all at once. Focus on one promise each day so that you make all seven promises to yourself each week. Do this each day for one year; it will be the best daily one minute you ever invest in yourself.

Repeat each day's promise to yourself at least four times—morning, afternoon, evening, and right before bed. At first, you'll probably hear that nagging little voice in the back of your head telling you how stupid you look. Ignore it—the inner critic is easily bored and will eventually go away. But now it's going to get even tougher, at least temporarily. You'll begin to experience what psychologists call cognitive dissonance, which is trying to hold two incompatible beliefs simultaneously. Cognitive dissonance is a painful emotional state; a form of mental illness.

When you've been promising yourself to be responsible, accountable, and determined but then catch yourself procrastinating, making excuses, and giving up, you're experiencing cognitive dissonance. At that point, one of two things *must* happen: Either you take the easy way out and stop making the promises, or you change your attitudes and behaviors in such a way as to start keeping the promises. When you do that, you will start to get better results. Now you're over the hump, and repeating the promises becomes an easy and pleasurable habit, because it's self-reinforcing.

The Self-Empowerment Pledge

Seven Simple Promises That Will Change Your Life

Monday's Promise: Responsibility

I will take complete responsibility for my health, my happiness, my success, and my life, and will not blame others for my problems or predicaments.

Tuesday's Promise: Accountability

I will not allow low self-esteem, self-limiting beliefs, or the negativity of others to prevent me from achieving my authentic goals and from becoming the person I am meant to be.

Wednesday's Promise: Determination

I will do the things I'm afraid to do, but which I know should be done. Sometimes this will mean asking for help to do that which I cannot do by myself.

Thursday's Promise: Contribution

I will earn the help I need in advance by helping other people now, and repay the help I receive by serving others later.

Friday's Promise: Resilience

I will face rejection and failure with courage, awareness, and perseverance, making these experiences the platform for future acceptance and success.

Saturday's Promise: Perspective

Though I might not understand why adversity happens, by my conscious choice I will find strength, compassion, and grace through my trials.

Sunday's Promise: Faith

My faith and my gratitude for all that I have been blessed with will shine through in my attitudes and in my actions.

You can download a slide show on The Self-Empowerment Pledge at www.JoeTye.com.

Appendix 3
Study Questions

These questions will help you apply the lessons of *All Hands on Deck* to the challenge of promoting a culture of ownership where you work. It is important to note that you do not have to be the CEO to have an impact on the culture of the place where you work. Anyone can make a difference. As Walt told Corey, "If you can dream it, you can do it."

Question #1: How does your organization currently reflect the four essential elements of a culture of ownership that Corey described to his bankers? What would an outsider, or a new employee, say about the level of commitment, engagement, passion, and pride where you work? How would they see it in your attitudes and behavior and in those of your co-workers?

Question #2: Using the structure described in Appendix 1 on the invisible architecture of an organization, how would you draw a cultural blueprint for your organization (1) as it is now and (2) as it would look in the ideal state? How far apart is the current reality from the ideal vision, and what would have to happen to bring the two closer together?

Question #3: In the introduction, I commented on how many organizations tolerate complaining, finger-pointing, passive-aggressiveness, and other forms of toxic emotional negativity in the way we once tolerated cigarette smoking. How does your organization do when it comes to fostering an emotionally positive and spiritually uplifting workplace environment? What more could be done to eradicate toxic emotional negativity in the way most places have now eradicated toxic cigarette smoke?

Question #4: After reading the seven simple promises of *The Self-Empowerment Pledge* in Appendix 2, ask yourself how much better your life would be—personally, professionally, financially, and spiritually—if you yourself were to make the commitment to live those promises each day of the week. Now imagine how different your workplace would be if everyone shared that.

Question #5: What do you make of the "creative insubordination" of Richard Drew at 3M or of Mari Colladay in this story? Would tolerance of "loose cannons" or "Skunk Works" like this be tolerated in your organization? Should they be? Would you be the sort of person who could engage in creative insubordination if you were sure that what you were doing was the right thing?

Question #6: Walt warned Corey against being a "yes, but man" who always found reasons to not do something; what barriers and objections might you expect to building a culture of ownership in your organization? How would you overcome the barriers and counter the objections?

Bibliography

These are the references I used to learn more about the legendary business leaders who are featured in *All Hands on Deck*. To the extent possible, words spoken by these leaders in this book are paraphrased, or in several cases, directly quoted from one of these sources. In any event, every effort has been made to assure that their comments are consistent with what they said in other contexts. The bibliography also includes a listing of general books on the subject of creating culture that have influenced my thinking and that I hope will influence yours as well. I've included this extended bibliography in hopes that you will be inspired to learn more about building a culture of ownership and about the leaders who have shown us how it's done.

Walt Disney

Barrier, Michael. *The Animated Man: A Life of Walt Disney*. Berkeley: University of California Press, 2007.

Cockerell, Lee. *Creating Magic: 10 Common Sense Leadership Strategies from a Life at Disney*. New York: Broadway Business, 2008.

Gabler, Neal. *Walt Disney: The Triumph of American Imagination*. New York: Alfred A. Knopf, 2006.

Lee, Fred. *If Disney Ran Your Hospital: 9 1/2 Things You Would Do Differently*. Bozeman, MT: Second River Healthcare Press, 2004.

Smith, Dave, comp. *The Quotable Walt Disney*. New York: Disney Enterprises, 2007.

Williams, Pat, and Jim Denney. *How to Be Like Walt: Capturing the Disney Magic Every Day of Your Life*. Deerfield Beach, FL: Health Communications, 2004.

Henry Ford

Grandin, Greg. *Fordlandia: The Rise and Fall of Henry Ford's Forgotten Jungle City*. New York: Henry Hold & Company, 2009.

Watts, Steven. *The People's Tycoon: Henry Ford and the American Century*. New York: Vintage Books, 2009.

Thomas Watson

Gerstner, Louis V. *Who Says Elephants Can't Dance? Leading a Great Enterprise through Dramatic Change*. New York: HarperCollins, 2005.

Maney, Kevin. *The Maverick and His Machine*. Hoboken, NJ: John Wiley & Sons, 2003.

Watson, Thomas Jr. *A Business and Its Beliefs: The Ideas That Helped Build IBM*. New York: McGraw Hill, 1963, 2003.

Watson, Thomas, Jr., and Peter Petre. *Father, Son & Co.: My Life at IBM and Beyond*. New York: Bantam Books, 1990, 2000.

Robert Wood Johnson

Biggers, John David. *Human Relations in Modern Business: A Guide for Action Sponsored by American Business Leaders*. New York: Prentice-Hall, 1949.

Foster, Lawrence. *A Company That Cares*. New Brunswick, NJ: Johnson & Johnson, 1986.

———. *Robert Wood Johnson: The Gentleman Rebel*. State College, PA: Lillian Press, 1999.

Johnson, Robert. *Bob Johnson Talks It Over*. New Brunswick, NJ: Johnson & Johnson, 1949.

Ray Kroc

Facella, Paul, and Adina Green. *Everything I Know about Business I Learned at McDonald's: The 7 Leadership Principles That Drive Breakout Success*. New York: McGraw Hill, 2009.

Harris, Patricia Sowell. *None of Us Is as Good as All of Us: How McDonald's Prospers by Embracing Inclusion and Diversity*. Hoboken, NJ: John Wiley & Sons, 2009.

Jones, Roland. *Standing Up & Standing Out*. Nashville: World Solutions, 2006.

Kroc, Ray, and Robert Anderson. *Grinding It Out: The Making of McDonald's*. Chicago: Contemporary Books, 1977.

Love, John. *McDonald's behind the Arches*. New York: Bantam Books, 1986, 1995.

McDonald's Corporation. *McDonald's @ 50*. Chicago: Imagination Publishing, 2005.

Ozersky, Josh. *The Hamburger: A History*. New Haven, CT: Yale University Press, 2008.

Bill Hewlett and Dave Packard

Malone, Michael S. *Bill & Dave: How Hewlett and Packard Built the World's Greatest Company*. New York: Portfolio, 2007.

Packard, David. *The HP Way: How Bill Hewlett and I Built Our Company*. New York: HarperCollins, 1995, 2005.

Mary Kay Ash

Ash, Mary Kay. *Mary Kay on People Management*. New York: Warner Books, 1984.

————. *The Mary Kay Way: Timeless Principles from America's Greatest Woman Entrepreneur*. Hoboken, NJ: John Wiley & Sons, 2008.

————. *You Can Have It All*. Rocklin, CA: Prima Publishing, 1995.

Underwood, Jim. *More Than a Pink Cadillac: Mary Kay Inc.'s 9 Leadership Keys to Success*. New York: McGraw Hill, 2002.

Ortega-Hennessy, Gillian. *It's Not Where You Start, It's Where You Finish! The Success Secrets of a Top Member of the Mary Kay Independent Sales Force*. Hoboken, NJ: John Wiley & Sons, 2005.

William McKnight

3M Company. *Our Story So Far: Notes from the First 75 Years of 3M Company*. St. Paul: Minnesota Mining and Manufacturing Company, 1977.

Comfort, Mildred Houghton. *William McKnight, Industrialist: A Biographical Sketch of the Chairman of the Board, Minnesota Mining and Manufacturing Company*. Men of Achievement. Minneapolis: T. S. Denison, 1962.

Gundling, Ernest. *The 3M Way to Innovation: Balancing People and Profit*. New York: Kodansha International, 2000.

Huck, Virginia. *Brand of the Tartan: The 3M Story*. New York: Appelton-Century-Crofts, 1955.

Courage quotes on Post-it Notes are drawn from: Tye, Joe. *Never Fear, Never Quit: A Story of Courage and Perseverance*. New York: Delacorte Press, 1997.

Millard Fuller

Baggett, Jerome. *Habitat for Humanity: Building Private Homes, Building Public Religion*. Philadelphia: Temple University Press, 2001.

Fuller, Millard. *More Than Houses*. Nashville: Word Publishing, 2000.

Youngs, Bettie. *The House That Love Built*. Charlottesville, VA: Hampton Roads Publishing Company, 2007.

General

Abrashoff, Michael. *It's Your Ship*. New York: Warner Business Books, 2002.

Blonchek, Robert, and Martin O'Neill. *Act Like an Owner: Building an Ownership Culture*. New York: John Wiley & Sons, 1999.

Branham, Leigh. *Keeping the People Who Keep You in Business*. New York: AMACOM, 2001.

Chaleff, Ira. *The Courageous Follower*. San Francisco: Berrett-Koehler Publishers, Inc., 1995, 2003.

Collins, James, and Jerry Porras. *Built to Last: Successful Habits of Visionary Companies*. New York: HarperCollins, 1994.

Collins, Jim. *Good to Great*. New York: HarperCollins, 2001.

Covey, Stephen M.R., and Rebecca Merrill. *The Speed of Trust: The One Thing That Changes Everything*. New York: Free Press, 2006.

Csikszentmihalyi, Mihaly. *Good Business: Leadership, Flow, and the Making of Meaning*. New York: Penguin Group, 2003.

Freiberg, Kevin, and Jackie Freiberg. *Guts! Companies That Blow the Doors off Business-as-Usual*. New York: Doubleday, 2004, 2005.

Healey, Joe. *Radical Trust: How Today's Great Leaders Convert People to Partners*. Hoboken, NJ: John Wiley & Sons, 2007.

Heskett, James L. *Ownership Quotient: Putting the Service Profit Chain to Work for Unbeatable Competitive Advantage*. Cambridge, MA: Harvard Business School Press, 2008.

Kaye, Beverly, and Sharon Jordan-Evans. *Love 'Em or Lose 'Em: Getting Good People to Stay*. San Francisco: Berrett-Koehler Publishers, 2005.

McGuire, John, and Gary Rhodes. *Transforming Your Leadership Culture*. San Francisco: Jossey-Bass, 2009.

Pfeffer, Jeffrey. *The Human Equation: Building Profits by Putting People First*. Cambridge, MA: Harvard Business School Press, 1998.

Reichheld, Frederick. *Loyalty Rules! How Today's Leaders Build Lasting Relationships*. Boston: Harvard Business School Press, 2001.

Sanders, Dan. *Built to Serve: How to Drive the Bottom Line with People-First Practices*. New York: McGraw Hill, 2008.

Stack, Jack, and Bo Burlingame. *A Stake in the Outcome: Building a Culture of Ownership for the Long-Term Success of Your Business*. New York: Doubleday, 2002, 2003.

Stubblefield, Al. *The Baptist Health Care Journey to Excellence: Creating a Culture That WOWs!* Hoboken, NJ: John Wiley & Sons, 2005.

Yerkes, Leslie. *Fun Works: Creating Places Where People Love to Work*. San Francisco: Berrett-Koehler Publishers, 2001.

About the Author

Joe Tye is CEO and Head Coach of Values Coach, Inc., which provides consulting, training, and coaching on values-based leadership and cultural transformation for hospital, corporate, and association clients. Joe earned a master's degree in hospital administration from the University of Iowa and an MBA from the Stanford Graduate School of Business, where he was class co-president. He is the author or coauthor of 10 previous books. He is a passionate keynoter and seminar leader with a powerfully important message for today's world. Prior to founding Values Coach in 1994, Joe was chief operating officer for a large community teaching hospital. Joe and his wife, Sally, have two adult children. They live on a small farmstead in Iowa, and their second home is a tent in the Grand Canyon.

Services from Values Coach Inc.

At Values Coach our mission is transforming people through the power of values and transforming organizations through the power of people. Our services include:

- Consulting on cultural transformation and creating a cultural blueprint™ for the invisible architecture™ of your organization.
- Training programs on values-based life and leadership skills with our 60-module course for *The Twelve Core Action Values*™. Participation in Values Coach courses has been a life-changing experience for many.
- Retreat facilitation to review and revitalize an organization's values, vision, and purpose—and leadership's commitment to achieving big goals.
- Joe Tye is available for keynotes, seminars and workshops for building a culture of ownership on a foundation of values.

Take "The Ownership Challenge" at
www.JoeTye.com.
Values Coach Inc.
400 Jordan Creek Plaza
P.O. Box 490
Solon, IA 52333-0490
319-624-3889
www.Values-Coach.com

Joe Tye's Speaking Topics

Joe is available for keynotes, workshops, and leadership retreats. He tailors each program to the audience and the goals of the organization, but these are his most popular topics:

All Hands on Deck: Building a Culture of Ownership on a Foundation of Values

Designing the Invisible Architecture: Why Values, Culture, and Emotional Climate Matter More than Bricks and Mortar

The Florence Challenge: From Accountability to Ownership in Healthcare

Never Fear, Never Quit: Cultural Toughness for Challenging Times

Winning the War with Yourself: Practical Strategies for Personal and Professional Success

The Twelve Core Action Values (this 60-module course is available as a 2-day leadership training program and as a longer-term cultural transformation initiative)

Call the Values Coach office at 800-644-3889 (319-624-3889) or contact your favorite speaker's bureau. Go to www.JoeTye.com to check Joe's calendar, topic details, and fee schedule.